Summer Favorites

C O O K B O O K

By Monica Musetti-Carlin and
Mary Elizabeth Roarke

COUNTRY COMFORT: SUMMER FAVORITES

Hatherleigh Press is committed to preserving and protecting the natural resources of the Earth. Environmentally responsible and sustainable practices are embraced within the company's mission statement.

Hatherleigh Press is a member of the Publishers Earth Alliance, committed to preserving and protecting the natural resources of the planet while developing a sustainable business model for the book publishing industry.

This book was edited and designed in the village of Hobart, New York. Hobart is a community that has embraced books and publishing as a component of its livelihood. There are several unique bookstores in the village. For more information, please visit www.hobartbookvillage.com.

Library of Congress Cataloging-in-Publication Data is available.
978-1-57826-384-4

Country Comfort: Summer Favorites is available for bulk purchase, special promotions, and premiums. For information on reselling and special purchase opportunities, call 1-800-528-2550 and ask for the Special Sales Manager.

Cover design by Nick Macagnone
Interior design by Nick Macagnone

10 9 8 7 6 5 4 3 2 1
Printed in the United States

DISCLAIMER
Any similarities to existing recipes are purely coincidental.

The summer book is dedicated to my late husband Dennis and my son Matt, in memory of all of the wonderful summer adventures that we shared together; and to my Aunt Dotty and Uncle Bob, who hosted many a family barbeque in their Long Island backyard when we were kids. We were always starved by the time we had arrived, because my dad, Bill, got lost on the way from the city every single time.

Monica

I dedicate this book to my mom and dad, for sharing their love of baking and cooking; to my daughter, Nicole, for sharing her culinary passion and expertise; and to my husband Dennis and our other children Elizabeth, Dennis, and Christian: thank you for your constant love and support.

Mary Elizabeth

We would especially like to thank our dedicated editor Anna Krusinski, for her initial and continued support throughout the process of writing our books. Her vision for our book complemented our own, and we could not see ourselves doing it without her.

Monica and Mary Elizabeth

———————

Thanks to Chef Nicole Roarke for putting into words our suggestions for the Chef's Tips section.
Thank you to all our creative home cooks who shared their families' favorite recipes.
Thank you for supporting our efforts and sending out our recipe request to your network of chefs:
MaryKate Roberts, the French Culinary Institute, New York, NY
Chef Mick Gehnrich, the Culinary Academy, Syosset, NY
Chef Michael S. Meshel, New York Guild of Chefs, New York, NY
Career Services, Institute of Culinary Education (ICE), New York, NY

Table of Contents

Foreword by Dan Glickberg   vii

Note to the Reader by Mary Elizabeth and Monica   ix

Introduction:
Passing on Traditions Through Food   xi

Part I: 1
Breakfast and Brunch   3

Part II: 25
Lunch   27

Part III: 69
Appetizers and Beverages   71

Part IV: 97
Entrées and Sides   99

Part V: 133
Desserts   135

Tips for a Well-Stocked Pantry   157

Grilling Tips   160

Chef's Tips by Chef Nicole Roarke   164

Baker's Tips   170

Menu Planner by Chef Nicole Roarke and Mary Elizabeth   172

Request for Future Submissions   177

Resources   178

About the Author   179

Index   180

Foreword

We live in an advanced technological age, an age of globalization that brings people from around the world closer together. Through today's technology, I can see what my high school friend is having for breakfast in Japan as I talk to him on Skype. I am privy to the restaurant in Boston that my college friend chooses for lunch as he checks in on Facebook. I can broadcast where I am going to dinner to my followers on Twitter (in 140 characters or less, of course).

With all of these technological advancements, I find it fascinating that food is trending in the opposite direction, towards localization. Countless markets and restaurants are now looking for as many local foods as they can find. Peruse the aisles of your food market and you are bound to run into produce that is marked with the distinction of being locally grown. It might even state how many miles it traveled to get into your shopping cart. Restaurants pride themselves on serving locally-sourced beef, seafood, and vegetables—now commonly known as "farm to table". Some even rely solely on local foods, changing their menus daily depending on what is available.

To me, no season encourages local eating the way summer does. For this reason alone, summer has always been my very favorite time of year for cooking. After all, what's better than firing up your grill and pulling the fresh crop from your garden to feed your family and friends? Not even the latest technology can replace that.

Spending my summers in Montauk, the eastern-most tip of Long Island, I have many fond memories of summer meals. My father and I would pass the days on his boat fishing for fluke, striped bass, cod, or yellowfin tuna. Most of our family dinners were built around the day's catch. Fresh salads and grilled vegetables would complete the meal, with lettuce and vegetables selected earlier that day from a local farmstand. Summer is the perfect time to embrace the inner chef in us all.

Needless to say, it brought back many great memories when Mary Elizabeth and Monica asked that my chef, Mitchel London, and I participate in this recipe book. Read on and you will be amazed to find countless recipes to help make your perfect summer meal. Food is all about individual preferences, so take the time to put your own personal touch on these recipes, adding and subtracting ingredients at your will. And while you're at it, take the time this summer to savor the fresh food all around you, enjoyed best in the company of family and friends.

—*Dan Glickberg*

Note to the Reader

We have been looking forward to writing this book for quite some time. Since the beginning of our project years ago, so many people have been waiting for their turn to pass on their traditional family favorites. Among them are many talented foodies and chefs, some of whom we have had the pleasure of meeting at our cooking demonstrations and book signings.

Both of us are native to New York, so we grew up with summers spent picnicking at parks or on one of the beautiful beaches that line the shores. Not only were outdoor summer activities plentiful, but so were fresh produce from local farm stands and seafood from the waters that bathed us on all sides.

Summer is an extra special time for Monica, because it evokes so many wonderful memories of backyard barbecues, outings to the beach, camping trips, and long summer vacations with her husband Dennis and their son Matthew. Whenever they traveled, they sampled the local fare and brought home with them flavors that one could only replicate through experience. Some of their favorite summer seafood finds included lobsters from Maine boiled in seawater, haddock from New Hampshire, cod from Cape Cod, and freshly caught Long Island clams to make chowders or to eat freshly opened with tangy cocktail sauce and lemon (or simply piled onto the grill, topped with lemon butter sauce). When visiting North Carolina, they discovered a barbeque joint that served pulled pork and ribs so succulent that friends back home in New York begged them to bring some back. On their summertime excursions, they also loved finding new and fresh desserts such as Blueberry Pie from Maine (page 153) and blackberry pie from Washington. Of course, there are also plenty of favorites to be found right at home, including homemade Italian Lemon Ice (page 149) from her cousin's ninety-year-old uncle and slow-cooked ribs that are "just fall-off-the-bone good," waiting to be devoured at her own backyard barbeques. Memories are always enhanced by great food with our family and friends, but can also strengthen bonds with total strangers that we meet along the way through meals shared during our travels.

Since Monica's husband passed away, her summers are more often spent at home, where she entertains friends and family by the pool, and enjoys tending to her beloved flower and vegetable gardens. She finds great joy in picking summer tomatoes, berries, and herbs fresh from her garden, and then tossing them onto the grill to share at the picnic table on the patio. These cherished summer days help Monica to create new memories and traditions right in her own backyard.

For Mary Elizabeth, her fondest summer recipes go back to her childhood. Each year, she looks forward to baking her Mom's Blueberry Picnic Cake (page 21) with berries from one of the many pick-your-own blueberry patches on Long Island. Another favorite is her dad's signature Sicilian Summer Pasta Sauce (page 125), using fresh mint grown wild in her garden.

In addition to recipes from people across the nation, you will find some of our own recipes, which we have carefully selected from our personal recipe boxes to share with you and your families. As always, our recipes are healthy and incorporate fresh fruits, vegetables, and herbs in most cases. Our hope is you will find new favorites that you can pass down to future generations in your family or share with your circle of friends during the lazy days of summer.

Introduction:
Passing on Traditions Through Food

Summertime pleasures include warm breezes and blue skies catching fireflies, and daydreaming poolside as the day turns to night when fireworks explode every Fourth of July.

The days of summer, officially beginning Memorial Day weekend and running through to Labor Day, bring with them so many fun-filled activities. Country fairs are held across the nation with contests for the best homemade preserves, pies, chili, and corndogs. Small-town carnivals arrive, offering kids the chance to brave their first Ferris wheel or roller coaster. Parades march through the streets to commemorate our country's heroes, eventually culminating in a baseball game and weenie roast in every backyard. Picnics in the park can become a daily activity, complete with games of Frisbee, bike rides, and a leisurely lunch of fried chicken and cucumber salad while sitting on the grass under a shady tree. Evenings bring concerts under the stars, with a bottle of wine, cheese, and fresh fruit. Of course, one can never forget summer camping trips on the lake, roasting marshmallows, and having a family sing-a-long after a day of hiking and canoeing. This is outdoor living at its best.

Children and adults alike can remember sunny days that we never wanted to end. Whether at home firing up the grill between volleyball bouts or out at the beach on a beautiful day to catch fresh fish for dinner, summer holds a special magic that we look forward to every year.

With the warmer weather, we eat according to the season, changing the foods we eat and the ways that we prepare them. On Memorial Day weekend, the first thought that comes to mind is a barbeque with loved ones. All-American favorites such as grilled ribs and chicken, hot dogs, hamburgers, and shish-kabobs adorn many a table throughout the summer. Heavy lasagnas are replaced with lighter salads like Monica's mom, Betty's, Macaroni Salad (page 47), Potato Salad (page 46), and Mary Elizabeth's Cole Slaw (page 44). For dessert, frozen treats such as sorbet and ice cream help keep everyone cool.

Monica's barbeques have changed quite a bit since her earliest memories of charcoal-grilled hamburgers that bore a frightening resemblance to hockey pucks. She likes to think of that as a transitional time in the world of modern-day grilling, when most newly suburban families first tried their hands at the art. With today's high-tech gas grills, charcoal often takes a back seat, though Monica still likes to use it for certain dishes to create a real old-fashioned flavor.

Thanks to the cultural diversity that is so prevalent in the United States and the availability of different spices from around the world, we as cooks can now easily transform flavors from Creole to Southern, from Middle Eastern to the West Indies to Eastern Indian, or from Texas barbeque to Louisiana barbeque. This vast variety in flavors also helps us to incorporate so many different ways to enhance traditional dishes.

Using marinades to tenderize meats or spicy rubs to permeate them can expand anyone's grilling techniques to gourmet proportions. Simple techniques such as using hickory smoke or prepared wood chips can quickly and easily add spectacular flavor to dishes. The same can be accomplished by soaking a batch of chicken in brine infused with spices, and then grilling or frying it. Each technique has its own allure and is sure to keep your guests coming back for more during the glorious season of summer.

At the end of your meal, a fresh fruit platter is perfect during the summer months. Across our country, we are blessed with an abundance of local farms just bursting with orchards and fields of watermelons, peaches, plums, and cherries, sundrenched and ripe for picking. Our Long Island east-end boasts fresh strawberries in July: colorful jewels welcomed by strawberry festivals and delightful music. You can pick your own in the fields or purchase crates to bring home. Summers in the Hamptons, where you can still see locals and vacationers walking, carrying an empty champagne glass with a fresh strawberry in it, ready to be filled at a neighbor's party. Red, white, and blue cakes for the Fourth of July grace many a table with American Flags made out of blueberries, raspberries, and, of course, strawberries, nestled on a platform of homemade whipped cream.

Summertime is best enjoyed when overflowing with fun-filled times with friends and family, cooking together, playing together, and staying together. Each day is another opportunity to keep heart-felt traditions alive for yet another season. Simple pleasures like swimming, barbequing, and singing become happy memories that will be shared and passed on to the next generations.

Part I

BREAKFAST AND BRUNCH

BREAKFAST AND BRUNCH

Waking up to nature's chorus is one of life's most rewarding moments. The birds sing out to greet each new day, and make us their willing audience. Blue jays, cardinals, house finches, and red-breasted robins soar overhead as they search out their next meal, and bees buzz about the garden, flitting from flower to flower and hovering over each clover for a morning treat. Dragonflies zip back and forth above the pool, dancing to their own tune, while hummingbirds grace us for a second, wings flapping with infinite speed, and disappearing as quickly as they came. Such is a summer morning, the quieting backdrop to our busy lives.

Breakfast is served with iced coffee, enjoyed while sitting peacefully out on the patio before the sun is too high and the weather too hot. It is such a pleasure to be outdoors, even for a little while, before going off to work each day. On most mornings, Monica picks fresh raspberries from her garden to eat by the handful or with cereal. When the harvest is at its peak in July, it is always a race with the birds to pick them all. She serves her raspberries daily for crepes, sauces, cakes, and fruit salads, and freezes extra for use throughout the summer in drinks and special dishes. Garden blueberries are also a daily treat, especially when used in Mary Elizabeth's friend, Carol's, Blueberry Lime Jam (page 23). When cherries are in season, Monica buys pounds of them and freezes them right away. You can eat them like candy or use in Cherry Pies (page 151) and sauces.

Checking the garden to see what is ready to be picked becomes a daily ritual during the summer. Tomatoes and peppers for a Spanish omelet, blueberries for a smoothie, and basil for a cream cheese spread all complement a lovely breakfast. A walk down the road to a neighbor's house can be like a walk through the Garden of Eden, resulting in homemade honey to drizzle on cinnamon French toast or fresh eggs in pastel colors from chickens that an old friend is raising on the next block.

To add to the sentiments of summer and make the start of your day even more pleasant, adorn your table with freshly cut roses in summery vases. Taking a few meditative moments over a delicious breakfast helps keep you on track to what is important in your life. Sharing that time with family is just as nice, and can offer a chance to teach your children how to pick snippets from the garden for your meal. Talking quietly together in a serene setting before rushing off heightens the quality of your time together.

Bird's Nest Eggs

Serves 4

When company stays the weekend at my house in the summer, I like them to feel as though they are staying in a quaint bed and breakfast. I get up really early before everyone else to prepare a special breakfast incorporating what I have picked from the garden. I raise the umbrella over the table out in the yard to shade us from the sun, and sip my own coffee blend laced with cinnamon, relaxing by the glistening blue of my pool as I wait for my sleepy guests to come down one by one to enjoy the day with me. Here are a couple of our favorite egg dishes. Serve with a basket of breads and fresh fruit on the side.

Story by Monica

9- by 11 ½-inch baking pan with enough water to fill ⅛-¼ of the way up
4 individual Pyrex® custard dishes
8 eggs, separated
4 tablespoons salted butter
1-2 cups seasoned bread crumbs
Sea salt and freshly cracked black pepper to taste

Butter individual Pyrex® custard dishes and sprinkle on the bottom with bread crumbs. Beat egg whites until very stiff. Place ¼ of the beaten egg whites into each dish. Make a little hollow in the center of each dish and place 2 egg yolks per person. Place in a baking pan. Bake uncovered at 325°F or just until egg whites are firm (about 15 minutes). Serve immediately.

Bread Crumbs

Leftover ends of breads or 1 small loaf of bread, sliced
Dried herbs, ground very fine (3 tablespoons parsley,
1 tablespoon basil, 1 teaspoon garlic, 1 teaspoon onion powder,
½ teaspoon paprika)
Salt and freshly ground black pepper to taste

Bake bread in a 300°F oven for about 15 minutes. You may have to turn bread once or twice before it is fully dry enough to grate/grind. Use large slices if grating by hand or break bread up into small pieces and process to your desired coarseness in a food processor or blender. Once ground, mix in herbs, paprika, and salt and pepper to taste. Shake together in a plastic bag until fully mixed.

Making Fresh Breadcrumbs

Freeze leftover ends of bread until you have enough to make breadcrumbs. Store unused breadcrumbs in plastic containers in the refrigerator for up to 1 week. Any kind of bread will do. You can also mix and match breads, adding a fuller flavor to your crumbs. When mixing in herbs and spices, use whatever ones that your dish at hand calls for. You can also add in grated cheese like pecorino Romano or sesame seeds.

Garden Vegetable Omelet with Cheese

Serves 2-4

1 cup yellow onion, diced fine
2 small zucchini, sliced thin
½ cup mushrooms, sliced thin
1 clove garlic, diced very fine
2 tablespoons butter
6 eggs, beaten with 1 tablespoon water
1 medium tomato, chopped
1 sprig parsley, chopped very fine
1 cup cheddar cheese, shredded
Sea salt and freshly cracked black pepper to taste

Sauté onion, zucchini, mushrooms, and garlic in 1 tablespoon of butter for 3-4 minutes and set aside. Melt remaining butter in large frying pan, and pour in beaten eggs, constantly pushing the egg mixture toward the center of the pan so the uncooked egg continues to fill the pan and cook. Once mostly cooked, shake the pan to loosen and carefully turn over. Immediately place onion, zucchini, mushrooms, garlic, tomato, half of the parsley, and cheese in the center of the egg. Turn ½ of the egg over the other, covering the vegetables, and then press gently with a spatula. Once the cheese begins to melt, turn the egg once, turn again if needed, and serve once all the cheese is melted. Sprinkle while hot off the stove with the remaining parsley and cheese. Salt and pepper to taste. (As an alternative to sautéing, you can also put the zucchini, onion, mushrooms, and butter in a microwave-safe bowl, cover with plastic wrap, and cook on high for 3 minutes before adding to the omelet).

Lox, Eggs, and Onions

Serves 3

2 ounces softened cream cheese (optional)
1 tablespoon prepared white horseradish (optional)
2 tablespoons butter
½ yellow onion, sliced thin
¼ pound smoked Atlantic Salmon or Nova Scotia lox (small slices)
6 eggs, beaten with 1 tablespoon water
3 scallions (greens only), chopped
1 teaspoon parsley, finely chopped
2 tablespoons capers (optional)

Mix cream cheese and horseradish together and set aside. In 2 tablespoons of butter, sauté the onion until almost clear, add in the lox, and stir until the lox becomes almost opaque. Then add in scallions and parsley and immediately pour in the eggs. Move the omelet mixture to the center of the pan, allowing the remaining uncooked egg mixture to cook. Shake the pan to loosen, turn the egg over once, and then fold in half and serve once all the egg is cooked. Spoon the cream cheese mixture over the hot omelet, and then sprinkle with the capers.

Homemade Waffles

Serves 2-4

Another breakfast special at "Casa Carlin" is homemade waffles. Summer fruits like fresh strawberries, blueberries and raspberries make delightful toppings. I like to serve a choice of either Vermont maple syrup, fresh clover honey, or my friend, Miss Amy's, strawberry or beach plum preserves, which she sells at farmers markets throughout New York. Waffles can be challenging, but they are well worth the extra work. I own an antiquated waffle maker from the 1950s, which we had used to make giant waffles in our Park Slope kitchen for years, but recently purchased a smaller one that is much easier to maneuver. You can mix finely chopped nuts into the batter for a nice variation (I like chopped pecans). When using nuts, I opt for the maple syrup and fresh bananas and peaches. Follow the directions on a box of pancake and waffle mix or use mine below, which I got from one of my former residents when I was a recreational therapist.

Story by Monica

4 cups sifted flour
4 teaspoons baking powder
4 tablespoons sugar
1 teaspoon sea salt
4 eggs separated
4 cups milk
8-12 tablespoons melted butter

Sift dry ingredients. Beat egg whites until stiff and set aside. Beat egg yolks, add milk, and mix gently by hand with the dry ingredients. Add butter. Fold in the egg whites. Pour into a waffle iron, and since the sizes of waffle irons vary, follow the manufacturer's directions for timing.

Blueberry Whole-Wheat Muffins

Robin De Nicola *(Patchogue, NY)*
Makes 12 muffins

Robin is a personal trainer, and is one of the only people who I know who practices what she preaches by rarely deviating from maintaining a healthy diet and lifestyle. She would be the mom who brings a homemade dish to the high school football dinners so she could be sure it was made with healthy ingredients. She writes the fitness forum column in our local paper, and recently went on to publish *Rockin' Robin's Handbook to a Healthier Life*, where these recipes first appeared.

Story by Mary Elizabeth

⅔ cup oat bran
1⅓ cups whole-wheat flour
¼ cup honey
½ tablespoon stevia
3½ teaspoons baking powder
½ teaspoon baking soda
2 tablespoons cinnamon
½ teaspoon nutmeg
1 egg
8 ounces plus 1 tablespoon unsweetened applesauce
½ cup skim milk
1 teaspoon vanilla extract
1 cup blueberries or your favorite berries
Sprinkle of ground flaxseeds (optional)
Nuts (optional)

Preheat oven to 400°F. Spray 12 muffin tins with baking spray. Mix all the ingredients together. Pour into the muffin tins. Bake until a toothpick comes out clean for approximately 15-17 minutes. Cool on wire racks and then turn out into a basket.

Whole-Wheat Peaches-and-Cream Muffins

Robin De Nicola *(Patchogue, NY)*
Makes 12 muffins

1 cup whole-wheat flour
¾ cup quick-cook oats
⅓ cup oat bran
2½ teaspoons baking powder
1 tablespoon cinnamon
Sprinkle of ground flaxseed
1 cup skim milk
⅓ cup honey plus ½ tablespoon stevia
3 tablespoons applesauce
2 teaspoons vanilla extract
1 egg
1 cup fresh peaches, diced

Cream Filling
½ cup low-fat cream cheese, softened
1 tablespoon honey
¼ cup peaches, diced

Preheat oven to 350°F and spray 12 muffin tins with non-stick baking spray. Combine dry ingredients in a medium bowl. Mix well. Add milk, honey, stevia, applesauce, vanilla, and egg to the dry ingredients. Stir in peaches.

Cream Filling

In a separate bowl, stir cream cheese and honey until smooth. Blend the fruit. Spoon ½ of mixture into muffin tins. Place 1 teaspoon of cream cheese mixture in the center of each tin, and then cover with batter. Bake 20-25 minutes or until a toothpick comes out clean.

Créme Brûlée French Toast Topped with Fresh Strawberries

Serves 6-8

2 tablespoons dark or light corn syrup

1 stick unsalted butter

1 cup brown sugar, packed

5 eggs

1½ cups half-and-half

1 teaspoon vanilla extract

1 teaspoon orange liquor

1 teaspoon fresh orange zest

¼ teaspoon sea salt

1 loaf French bread cut into cubes (leave crust on)

½ pint fresh strawberries, hulled and thinly sliced

Generously spray bottom of 9- by 12-inch Pyrex® dish with non-stick baking spray. In a small saucepan, combine the corn syrup, butter, and brown sugar, and simmer until syrupy. Toss this mixture thoroughly with the bread cubes. Pour into the prepared Pyrex® dish. Set aside. In a large bowl, whisk together the eggs, half-and-half, vanilla extract, orange liquor, zest, and salt. Pour evenly over the bread and press down with the back of a spoon. Cover and refrigerate overnight. In the morning, bring the Pyrex® dish to room temperature while the oven preheats. Bake at 350°F uncovered for 45 minutes. Serve immediately with strawberries, syrup, and butter. This dish can also easily be reheated.

Vanilla Almond Multigrain French Toast Topped with Summer Berries

Kathleen White *(Blue Point, NY)*
Serves 4-6

Kathleen is a certified holistic health-and-fitness coach so she likes to use ingredients that are organic. Here is a recipe that she serves in the summer, which her family, friends, and clients rave about. She put a slightly different spin on this old-time favorite, making it extra healthy without taking away the enjoyment of eating it. When she first told me about this recipe, she remarked that she was surprised by how adding almond extract could make it taste so good. She also likes to sprinkle extra cinnamon on top with a very small amount of confectioners' sugar for added appeal and taste just before serving.

Story by Mary Elizabeth

French Toast
2 eggs
½ cup milk
¼ teaspoon cinnamon
½ teaspoon almond extract
½ teaspoon vanilla extract
Pinch of nutmeg
6-8 slices multi-grain or soft organic white bread
¼ cup walnuts or almonds, crushed
Agave nectar, to taste

Fresh Whipped Cream
1 cup heavy cream
1 cup sugar

French Toast

Beat eggs in a medium bowl. Add milk and stir vigorously with a fork until the milk and eggs are blended together. Add cinnamon, extracts, and nutmeg and stir until well blended into the eggs and milk.

Add a thin slice of butter into a preheated pan or griddle over low to medium flame or temperature.

Dip bread into the egg mixture, coating both sides. Scrape off excess mixture, leaving the bread with a film-like coating on the bread. Add to a pan or skillet. Turn over on the opposite side after about 30 seconds, slightly browning each side. Repeat this until all the mixture is gone.

Fresh Whipped Cream

Beat heavy cream and sugar together until thick and creamy.

Sprinkle nuts on top of the French toast with a tablespoon of whipped cream and a drizzle of agave nectar before serving.

French Toast Bake with Summer Berries

Lana Rae Armitage *(Portsmouth, RI)*
Serves 8

2½ sticks unsalted butter
1½ cups brown sugar
2 tablespoons cinnamon
2 (16 oz.) loaves good-quality cinnamon-swirl bread,
crusts removed
8 eggs
2 cups whole milk
2 teaspoons confectioners' sugar (optional)
1 cup assorted summer berries of your choice, washed (optional)

Preheat oven to 350°F. Spray a 9- by 12-inch glass oven-proof dish with baking spray.

Melt butter, and add brown sugar and cinnamon. Stir until thoroughly combined and pour into the prepared dish.

Layer all the bread in the dish. In a large bowl, beat eggs and milk together and pour over the bread. Push the bread down with the back of a large spoon so the bread is below the liquid. Cover with plastic wrap and refrigerate overnight. Remove the plastic wrap and bake uncovered for 40 minutes. Just before serving, cook under a broiler for 2 minutes until brown/crisp. Sprinkle with confectioners' sugar and assorted berries, if desired.

Crepes with Berry Toppings

Chef Andrea Glick *(Norfolk, NY)*
Serves 4-6

We met Chef Andrea at a food demonstration that we recently did at a culinary school, where she is a chef instructor. She also acted as a scribe and tested the recipes for A Return to Cooking, a cookbook by Chef Eric Ripert. Given her vast experience, we were thrilled when she offered to share a recipe with us.

Story by Mary Elizabeth

Crepes

1 cup all-purpose flour
1 tablespoon sugar
¼ teaspoon fine sea salt
3 eggs
1½ cups milk
2 tablespoon butter, melted
¼ teaspoon butter

Berries

2 tablespoons unsalted butter
2 tablespoons sugar
1 quart whole fresh blueberries or cleaned and quartered strawberries
Powdered sugar, for garnish (optional)

Crepes

Sift together the flour and salt. Whisk to aerate. Add the milk, and whisk to combine. Whisking constantly, add the egg mixture to the dry ingredients until combined. Add melted butter slowly and whisk to incorporate. Strain through a sieve to remove any lumps. Rest batter for at least an hour in the refrigerator.

In a 6-inch non-stick sauté pan over medium-high heat, heat ¼ teaspoon of butter and swirl until melted and distributed. Ladle 1 ounce of batter and swirl to distribute evenly. Cook for 1 minute or until it is browned. Flip the crepe and cook another minute or until browned. Stack and wrap in plastic film until ready to serve.

Berries

Heat the butter in a pan, add the sugar, and stir over medium-heat until caramelized. Add the berries and cook until the berries have started to break down and are syrupy.

To serve, fold two crepes into quarters and place on a plate. Spoon the berries over the crepes and garnish with powdered sugar, if desired.

Chef's Tip

The first crepe may be lost due to uneven pan heat. No worries: the next one will be beautiful, and you will not need to add any more butter to the pan due to the butter in the batter.

Cheese Filling

As an alternative you can add 2 tablespoons of Mary Elizabeth's cheese filing to the center of the crepe before folding.

1 (15 oz.) container whole milk ricotta, drained in a sieve

6 ounces cream cheese, softened

1 tablespoon all-purpose flour

1⅛ teaspoon cinnamon

3 tablespoons sugar

1 teaspoon vanilla

1 teaspoon lemon zest

To prepare cheese filling, beat ricotta cheese, cream cheese, flour, cinnamon, sugar, vanilla extract, and zest in a large bowl until blended.

Caramelized Onion and Gruyere Tart

Chef Geraldine Pollock *(Islip, NY)*
Serves 6-8

4 ounces bacon, cut into ¼-inch strips
4 ounces Spanish onions, julienne cut and caramelized (see note)
1 tablespoon extra virgin olive oil
6 ounces liquid egg
6 ounces heavy cream
2 tablespoons fresh parsley, chopped
4 ounces gruyere cheese, shredded
1 (9-inch) pre-made pie dough or homemade pâte brisée (see page 19)
Sea salt and freshly cracked black pepper to taste

Render bacon until crisp, and lay out on a paper towel to remove the grease. Set aside. Over high heat, pan-sear onions in olive oil until browned, and set aside to cool. In a stainless steel bowl, combine eggs, cream, parsley and salt and pepper, mixing well.

Set dough into an 8-inch pan and press down until dough has a 1-inch height. Place bacon, onions, and gruyere into the dough, and cover with the liquid egg mixture. Bake for 25 minutes at 375°F, or until the egg has set. Let sit for 10 minutes.

Serve immediately.

Chef's Tip

When food is sliced into even, thin "matchstick strips," it is called a julienne cut. Since the onion is round, cut off both ends, so, you have more control over it. This will also prevent the onion from rolling when you place it on the cutting board. To julienne-cut, angle your knife sharply and begin cutting into square pieces that resemble matchsticks.

Pàte Brisée

Chef Tricia Wheeler *(Columbus, OH)*
Makes 1 crust to cover 9-inch pie plate

> I first met Tricia at my daughter's graduation from the French Culinary Institute in New York City. She was graduating that day, as well, and was eager to get home to start her next venture. It was evident after a short conversation that she would go on to become very successful. Tricia is now the publisher and editor-in-chief of *Edible Ohio*.
>
> *Story by Mary Elizabeth*

1¼ cups flour
½ teaspoon sea salt
½ cup unsalted butter, cut into small pieces
5 tablespoons ice water

In a large bowl, sift together flour and salt. Add the butter and rub in using your fingertips until fine crumbs form. Alternatively, you can combine in the food processor. Slowly add the water, mixing until a crumbly dough begins to form (do not overwork the dough). Pinch a piece: it should hold together. If the dough is crumbly, add a little more water. If it is wet and sticky, add a little flour.

Push the dough with one hand away from you until the dough is smooth and pliable. Flatten the dough to a round disc, and wrap in plastic wrap. Chill for 2 hours or overnight. Leave to soften for 10 minutes at room temperature before rolling out. Lightly butter a 9- or 10-inch pie dish. On a lightly floured surface, roll out the dough to a thickness of 1/8-inch. Gently roll the pastry around the rolling pin, and then unroll over the pie dish, leaving a 1-inch overhang.

With floured fingers, press the overhang down slightly toward the base of the dish to reinforce the side; roll the rolling pin over the rim to cut off the excess. Dip the index finger and thumb of your left hand into ice water, and pinch a small section of the dough along the rim of the pie dish. Using the index finger of your right hand, "push" into the dough you are pinching (if you are left-handed, reverse the directions). Continue this motion until you have completed the entire rim. Prick the base with a fork and chill for 1 hour.

Sausage and Cheese Breakfast

Chef Geraldine Pollack *(Islip, NY)*

Serves 6

Every summer when we visit our friends, Tim and Carol's, second home in upstate New York, we look forward to waking to the aroma of freshly brewed coffee and this sausage and cheese dish baking in the oven. We always marvel at the novelty that the eggs were collected from the adorable, red chicken coop located outside their kitchen window!

Story by Mary Elizabeth

6 slices buttered bread (butter both sides)
1 pound breakfast sausages, removed from casing
6 ounces sharp cheddar cheese, grated
6 eggs
1 pint half-and-half
1 teaspoon sea salt

Place buttered bread in a 9- by 13-inch pan. Crumble 1 pound of cooked breakfast sausage over bread. Sprinkle cheese over the sausage. In a bowl, beat eggs with half-and-half and salt, pouring over the other ingredients. Cover in plastic wrap and refrigerate overnight. Bring to room temperature and bake in at 350°F in an oven for about 30 minutes.

Blueberry Picnic Cake

Lena T. Raiser *(Lynbrook, NY)*
Makes 24 (2-inch) squares

I often make my mom's recipe when we cater a brunch. It is a nice alternative to serving muffins or a traditional coffee cake. It cuts nicely into squares, and also travels well: two qualities that I always look for when choosing a recipe for a catering event. This buttery, sugary cake is always a hit.

Story by Mary Elizabeth

3 egg whites
3 egg yolks
½ cup whole milk
¼ cup sour cream
3 cups unsifted flour
2 cups sugar
2 sticks butter (soften 1 stick; melt 1 stick)
Zest from 1 lemon
½ teaspoon cinnamon
3 teaspoons baking powder
1 teaspoon sea salt
2 cups fresh blueberries
2 tablespoons raw sugar

Preheat oven to 350°F. In a small bowl, beat egg whites until dry and stiff. Set aside. In a large bowl, whisk egg yolks, milk, and sour cream. Set aside. In a third bowl, mix flour, sugar, and 1 stick of softened butter until pea-sized crumbs form. Remove 1 cup of the crumb mixture and set aside.

To the remaining flour mixture, add lemon zest, cinnamon, baking powder, and salt. Blend thoroughly with a mixer. Set aside.

Gradually add the flour mixture into the egg mixture until the flour is all mixed in. Fold the eggs gently into the batter.

Prepare a 9- by 13-inch glass pan. Spray bottom and sides of the pan generously with baking spray, and then line the bottom with a piece of parchment paper and spray the parchment.

Spread the batter into the pan, and then arrange blueberries in lines. Top evenly with the reserved crumb mixture. Bake at 350°F for 1 hour. As soon as you remove the cake from the oven, poke holes in the top using the bottom of a wooden spoon. Pour 1 stick of melted butter on top of the cake. Sprinkle with raw sugar (can be served warm or cold).

Blueberry Lime Jam

Carol Smith *(Bovina Center, NY)*
Makes 6 cups

> Every August when we start to hear people around town saying, "The blueberries are ripe," my husband Tim and I go to our favorite blueberry farm in the Catskill Mountains. Each year, we look forward to this glorious day. We pick the berries from morning until night, eating as many as we bring home. Over the next few days, we make blueberry jam and pies. This is one of my favorite days of the year. A farmer's wife gave me this recipe.

4½ cups ripe blueberries
1 package of dry pectin
5 cups sugar
⅓ cup freshly squeezed lime juice
1 tablespoon lime zest

Crush the berries with a potato masher, one layer at a time. Combine the crushed berries and the pectin in a large pot. Bring to a boil, stirring frequently. Add the sugar, stirring until dissolved. Stir in the lime juice and zest, and return to a boil. Boil for 1 minute, stirring constantly. Turn off the heat and skim the foam if needed.

Prepare the half-pint glass jars by running them through the dishwasher. Dry thoroughly, and then spoon jam into the jars, leaving a ¼-inch from the top. Cover with the rubber rings and screw the lid on (but not too snugly). Cool on a wire rack for 24 hours (as it cools, the vacuum seals itself). Once cooled, screw the lids on tightly before storing or giving away as gifts. Can be stored for 12 months, but best when eaten within 6 months.

The booklets that come with canning jars often have great tips for trouble-shooting.

Part II

LUNCH

LUNCH

We typically do not eat heavy lunches during the summer, primarily because it can be just too hot and uncomfortable, especially midday, when the sun is at its highest. A fresh salad served with Gazpacho (page 60) or a zesty North Fork Clam Chowder (page 61) is a tasty lunch choice that will satisfy your hunger without feeling too full. A Fairway Market's Lobster Roll (page 29) can also do the trick, making you feel as though you are on vacation in Maine, instead of at lunch during a workday. Monica likes to bring a leftover grilled hot dog or hamburger with her to work, making lunch a delight as she thinks back to yesterday's barbeque with the family. Mary Elizabeth savors her hot dogs with her dad's homemade sauerkraut.

Finding a nice spot to enjoy your afternoon break is just as important as the meal itself. If your job is near the water, find a nice dock or beachfront to sit and eat your lunch—you will feel like you are on a mini-vacation for an hour. If you work in a large office building, try finding a quiet spot hidden between the skyscrapers with fountains, flowers, and tables for you to relax and unwind.

Lunch at home during a pool party calls for a real crowd-pleaser. Make specially prepared grilled hamburgers, complete with hand-picked garden tomatoes, cucumbers, lettuce, and a Poppy Seed Dressing (page 52). A nice Italian Pasta Salad (page 64) or a side of Smoked Gouda Macaroni and Cheese (page 131) rounds out your meal, and a tall, icy glass of refreshing fresh-squeezed lemonade or homemade ginger ale hits the spot every time.

Relaxing and then having a swim to work off some of your lunch calories is as good a time as you could have at any resort, right in the comfort of your own home. Make your backyard an oasis with potted and hanging plants. Seasonal flowers like impatiens or petunias are a quick and inexpensive way to add color to your landscape and brighten your afternoons, which, in turn, brighten your spirit. Keep a pitcher of lemonade or iced water in a thermos to refill your glasses and stay cool while enjoying the warm sunshine and the good company of friends.

Fairway Market's Lobster Roll

Danny Glickberg and Chef Mitchel London *(New York, NY)*
Serves 4

In the summer of 2003, during Danny's sophomore year at college, he worked under Mitchel as a waiter in Fairway Market's Cafe & Steakhouse in New York City. After graduating, he returned to Fairway and learned that Mitchel no longer worked there, leading Danny to make the first major decision of his career. He brought Mitchel back, and together, they launched a video website in 2008. It featured one-minute food tips and cooking shorts. Realizing they had a growing audience, they began to do live demonstrations, and shortly thereafter, NBC taped them for weekly cooking segments shown during the five o'clock news. Fortunately, they shared several of their summer recipes with us.

Story by Mary Elizabeth

2 (2-pound) lobsters
4 ribs celery, diced
¼ cup chives, finely chopped
⅓ cup mayonnaise
1 pinch cayenne pepper
4 hot dog buns

Place 1 inch of water in a pot that is big enough to hold both lobsters or each lobster separately. Bring water to a rapid boil, and place the lobsters in the pot(s) and cover tightly. Lower the heat, but keep it high enough to maintain the water boiling. Steam the lobsters for about 15 minutes, but no more.

Remove the lobsters from the pot(s) and cool. Remove the meat from the shell and chill in the refrigerator. Do not rinse the meat under cool water to chill.

Shred the meat with your hands and place in a bowl. Add celery, chives, and mayonnaise, and blend together. Finish with a pinch of cayenne pepper. Toast and butter your buns and add the lobster salad evenly to them.

Deluxe Turkey Burgers

Tom Lamia *(Blue Point, NY)*
Serves 4

Mary Elizabeth and I met this lovely family at one of our book signings and tastings. They were really enthusiastic about sharing some of their family recipes with us. They sent along several dishes: one from their young daughter, and one from their grandpa. This is the one that we chose, because it was a great, virtually fat-free burger alternative on the grill.

Story by Monica

3 ounces extra virgin olive oil
2 ounces red wine vinegar
1 ounce Worcestershire sauce
2 teaspoons creamy dijon mustard
2 tablespoons fresh basil, chopped
2 teaspoons Bisquick®
1 small onion, chopped, or 2-3 garlic cloves, crushed
1½ pounds ground turkey
Bread crumbs to taste
Sea salt and paprika to taste

Make the marinade by mixing all the ingredients together (except the turkey, bread crumbs, and paprika). Pour in a 9- by 13-inch rectangular pan. Lightly make 4 equal-sized turkey patties by pressing them between your hands. Pat them gently into the marinade. Cover the pan with tin foil and put in the refrigerator for 2 hours. Turn the patties over a few times so the sides equally soak in the marinade. Discard the marinade and sprinkle each patty with bread crumbs and paprika. Grill on low, turning twice.

Memorial Day Hamburgers

Serves 10

Our first big barbeque of the year is always on Memorial Day weekend. After going to the parade in town, I rush home to start preparing for the family to arrive. I have the pool opened on May 1st so it is ready in time, although the kids and I are usually the only ones who will swim so early in the season. My menu is the one everybody craves, because it is reminiscent of our barbeques as kids: hamburgers, hot dogs, and potato and macaroni salads. I have added my mom's Italian pasta salad, my sister's baked beans, and always a big green salad. I like to make it fun at the table by serving chili for the hot dogs and interesting toppings for the burgers. Everyone's favorite is bacon with cheddar cheese and a slice of raw onion, so they are always on the grill. Yet I like to experiment, and below is one of my favorites.

Story by Monica

2 cups grape tomatoes, sliced
1 large red onion, finely chopped
2 tablespoons fresh mint, chopped very fine
2 tablespoons fresh parsley, chopped very fine
2 tablespoons balsamic vinegar
1 tablespoon extra virgin olive oil

2½ pounds chopped sirloin fashioned into burger patties (¼ pound per burger)
Teriyaki sauce to taste
1 pound applewood smoked bacon, cooked until crispy, not dry
1 pound crumbled Roquefort cheese
Whole-wheat buns

Marinate the tomatoes, onion, mint, parsley, balsamic vinegar, and olive oil, and set aside. Grill the burgers on low, adding a splash of teriyaki on each burger, turning them often, and being careful not to press out the juices. Right before they are ready to come off the grill, top with a teaspoon each of your marinated tomatoes, cooked applewood smoked bacon, and cheese. Remove when the cheese is fully melted, about 1 or 2 minutes. Serve on whole-wheat buns.

Labor Day Chili

Dorothy Acierno (Bayport, NY)
Serves 12

Every Labor Day, we would end the summer with a big chili party with our friends, whom we called the "Poker Club" on our boat, the Deama, docked at the Sayville Yacht Club. The boat, originally named the Marlin, was famous for having belonged to the Kennedys. Per my husband's instructions, I painted on our new name, which was supposed to be spelled "Diama," standing for my name and our children at the time. Yet I made a mistake and put an "e" instead of an "i." We just left it that way and laughed about it. When my daughter Patsy was born, she was upset that her name was not represented, and she wanted us to rename the boat, the "Princess Patsy". We did not change the name, and found out years later that "Deama" was Italian for a "woman God". Being a family with very strong women in it, we were delighted to hear that.

5 pounds beef brisket, chuck or any inexpensive cut of meat
1 large yellow onion, sliced
Vegetable oil for browning meat
3 tablespoons chili powder
1 tablespoon cayenne pepper flakes
2 (28 oz.) cans tomato puree

28 ounces water
1 (12 oz.) can, kidney beans
1 (8 or 12 oz.) jar sliced jalapeño peppers (optional)
1 pound cheddar cheese, shredded (optional)
Salt and freshly ground pepper to taste

Brown the meat on all sides in the vegetable oil, add the onion, cover, and cook as you would for a pot roast (at least 3 hours), until the meat is falling apart. Then shred the meat and add in the remaining ingredients in the order written above, except the jalapeños and cheese. Cook for about 1-1½ hours, stirring occasionally. If you desire a thinner consistency, add a little water; to make it a bit thicker, add a little tomato paste. Serve with jalapeño peppers and cheese on the side (optional).

Memorial Day Chili Dogs

Serves 10

This is another family favorite during our annual Memorial Day barbeque.

Story by Monica

Hot Dogs

20 good-quality garlicky hot dogs

1 pound cheddar cheese, shredded

Dark mustard

Chili

1 pound chopped sirloin

1 yellow onion, sliced

2 teaspoons oregano

3 teaspoons chili powder

1-2 teaspoons cumin

6 jarred jalapeño pepper rings, finely chopped (or ¼ fresh jalapeño pepper, chopped very fine)

1 (15 oz.) can crushed tomatoes, with the equivalent in water

1 (6 oz.) can tomato paste, with the equivalent in water

1 (19 oz.) can kidney beans, drained

Sea salt to taste

On the stove-top, brown the meat fully with the onions. Mix in oregano, chili powder, cumin, jalapeños, and salt. Then transfer to a larger pot, adding in the tomatoes and paste, water, and kidney beans. Cook 1-2 hours.

Grill your hot dogs and serve on whole-wheat buns. Top with hot chili and shredded cheese.

Grilled Fig, Brie, and Prosciutto Pizza

Chef Sonali Ruder *(New York, NY)*
Serves 8 (makes 2 small pizzas)

Dr. Sonali Ruder, a busy emergency room physician, decided to follow her passion for cooking and recently graduated from culinary school. Her main interest is in recipe writing, getting her start by entering cooking contests. Sonali's science background, precise and meticulous, blends beautifully with her creative side when she is designing and testing recipes at home with her husband, a fellow doctor and food lover.

Story by Mary Elizabeth

6 black mission figs, sliced into quarters
5 teaspoons balsamic vinegar, divided
1 ball prepared pizza dough, divided into 2 rounds
2 tablespoons all-purpose flour, for dusting
3 tablespoons olive oil, divided
8 ounces brie cheese, sliced
2 ounces prosciutto, sliced
2 ounces baby arugula leaves
Kosher salt and freshly cracked black pepper to taste

Preheat a gas or charcoal grill to medium-high heat.

Toss the figs with 2 teaspoons of balsamic vinegar in a small bowl. Set aside.

Working on a clean surface, roll each ball of dough out with a rolling pin (or stretch by hand) until the crust is ¼-inch thick. Dust with flour as needed if the dough sticks. Brush the dough with olive oil and gently place one on the grill. After 2-3 minutes, when the crust is set, gently flip it over using tongs. Brush the dough with olive oil, and then, working quickly, arrange half of the brie slices and figs evenly over the crust. Close the grill and cook for another 2-4 minutes until the cheese starts to melt and the figs are slightly softened. Remove the pizza from the grill and top with half of the prosciutto. Repeat the process with the remaining ball of dough and toppings.

Whisk 1 tablespoon of balsamic vinegar and 2 tablespoons of olive oil together in a medium bowl. Add the baby arugula and toss to combine. Season with salt and pepper to taste. Arrange the baby arugula on top of the pizzas. Cut the pizza into slices and serve warm.

Brooklyn's Cheesiest Dog

Chef Nick Suarez *(Brooklyn, NY)*
Serves 4

Nick specializes in taking classic American comfort dishes and giving them a modern twist. His claim to fame occurred when he won the 2009 Great Hot Dog Cook-Off and, subsequently, was challenged by Iron Chef Bobby Flay on the Food Network's Throwdown—and won. His recipe is called Brooklyn's Cheesiest Dog, and marries his famous bacon and leek macaroni and cheese with a hot dog.

Story by Mary Elizabeth

4 slices slab bacon, cut into lardons (thin strips, cut approximately ¼-inch thick)
2 tablespoons olive oil
2 leeks, chopped into ¼-inch slices
5 tablespoons salted butter, separated
3 tablespoons all-purpose flour
1½ cups whole milk, heated
8 ounces gruyere, grated
2 ounces parmigiano-reggiano, grated
Pinch cayenne pepper
Pinch ground nutmeg
¼ cup panko bread crumbs
¼ pound pasta (gemelli or elbow-shaped)
4 hot dog buns
4 hot dogs, all-beef with natural casing
2 tablespoons hot sauce
Fresh Italian parsley leaves, finely chopped
Sea salt and freshly cracked black pepper to taste

In a medium-sized saucepan over medium heat, sauté the bacon until brown and crispy. Remove the bacon from the pan and drain on paper towels. Discard the bacon fat. Put the olive oil into the same pan. Wash the chopped leeks thoroughly to remove any grit, and then drain. Put them into the pan with the olive oil and sauté until soft and wilted. Remove the leeks from the pan and set aside.

Make the *roux* by melting 3 tablespoons of butter in the saucepan, and then sprinkle with the flour, stirring to incorporate. Continue to cook it over medium heat for a few minutes. Whisk the warm milk into the roux and cook until it thickens. Fold in the grated gruyere and grated parmigiano, and season with salt and pepper to taste. Add a pinch of cayenne and a pinch of nutmeg. Set the sauce aside.

Bring a large pot of salted water to boil over medium heat for the pasta.

In a small fry pan, melt 1 tablespoon of butter and add the panko. Stir constantly until the crumbs are lightly toasted. Set aside.

Preheat the grill to medium.

Once the water is boiling, add the pasta and cook until al dente. Drain and gently fold the cooked pasta into the cheese sauce and keep warm. Fold in the reserved bacon and leeks.

Melt the remaining tablespoon of butter and brush it on the cut sides of the buns. Grill the hot dogs over the hottest part of the barbeque until they are brown, and toast the buns around the perimeter where the fire is cooler until you have light-golden grill marks. Put 1 hot dog into each bun and generously slather with the hot sauce. Top each hot dog with a generous portion of the pasta and cheese sauce. Sprinkle with the toasted panko and chopped parsley, and serve.

Brooklyn's Corniest Dog

Chef Nick Suarez *(Brooklyn, NY)*
Serves 4

3 slices thick-cut bacon, cut into small lardons (thin strips, cut approximately ¼-inch thick)
2 large onions, finely chopped
1 teaspoon kosher salt, divided
2 tablespoons canola oil
3 ears corn, kernels removed
½ teaspoon sugar
1 tablespoon fresh cilantro leaves, finely chopped
4 hot dogs
1 tablespoon piri-piri hot sauce or Tabasco sauce
4 potato buns
4 tablespoons salted butter, melted
2 tablespoons mayonnaise
2 tablespoons whole-grain mustard
¼ cup grated cotija cheese or parmesan
Pinch cayenne pepper
½ lime, quartered
Freshly cracked black pepper to taste

Bacon

Sauté the lardons in a frying pan over medium heat until the fat is rendered and the bacon is crispy. Reserve the bacon lardons for garnish and reserve the bacon fat for cooking the onions.

Caramelized Onions

Put the onions into the bacon fat, season with a ½ teaspoon of salt to draw out the moisture, and cook gently over medium heat until caramelized (about 20 minutes). Reserve.

Corn

Put 2 tablespoons of canola oil in a hot pan over medium heat. When the oil starts to smoke, add the corn kernels, ½ teaspoon of sugar, ½ teaspoon of kosher salt, and freshly ground pepper to taste. Sauté over high heat until the corn starts to caramelize, stirring frequently. Remove from the heat and add 1 tablespoon cilantro. Reserve for later.

Hot Dogs

Heat a grill to high. Put the hot dogs on the grill and sear until slightly charred. Brush lightly with hot sauce while still on the grill. Meanwhile, brush the inside of the buns with melted butter and arrange, butter-side-down, on the grill. Grill until lightly golden brown (about 30 seconds).

Thinly spread the mayonnaise and mustard on each bun. Put the hot dogs into the buns and sprinkle with a tablespoon of caramelized onions. Top with a tablespoon of lardons and 2 tablespoons of the corn mixture. Sprinkle each with ½ tablespoon of cotija cheese and a pinch of cayenne pepper. Squeeze a little lime on each hot dog and serve.

Grilled Vegetable Pitas

Chef Julian Bonilla, North Fork Country Club *(Cutchogue, NY)*
Serves 8

Balsamic Vinaigrette

1 teaspoon shallot, chopped
½ teaspoon garlic, chopped
1 tablespoon dijon mustard
½ teaspoon fresh thyme, chopped
½ teaspoon fresh rosemary, chopped
½ teaspoon fresh oregano, chopped
¼ cup balsamic vinegar
2 tablespoons cold water
1½ teaspoon kosher salt
½ teaspoon fresh cracked black pepper
2 teaspoons honey
¾ cup canola oil plus 2 ounces olive oil

Vegetables

1 zucchini, sliced on bias in ¼-inch thick slices
1 yellow squash, ¼-inch thick slices on bias
1 red pepper, cut into 1-inch strips
1 yellow pepper, cut into 1-inch strips
1 bunch asparagus, about 24 trimmed
2 Portobello mushrooms, sliced ¼-inch
1 medium eggplant, slice in ¼-inch thick rounds
1 carrot, sliced thinly on bias
6 pita bread pieces, split and brushed lightly with olive oil
12 slices fontina or similar cheese (muenster, gruyere, swiss, cheddar)
Sea salt and freshly cracked black pepper to taste

Balsamic Vinaigrette

Place all the ingredients in a bowl (except the oils), and mix well, then slowly drizzling in the oils.

Vegetables

Place the sliced vegetables in a bowl, adding enough vinaigrette to just coat them lightly. Then place the vegetables on a hot grill or barbeque, turning so as not to burn. Continue to cook until tender, remove, and season with salt and pepper.

Lightly grill the open-faced pitas. Place a portion of vegetables in each pita, covering with 2 slices of cheese and then lightly with foil. The heat of the vegetables will melt the cheese.

Plate with a small salad of mixed greens, tomatoes, and a little of the vinaigrette (there will be plenty).

Corn Salad

Christian David Raiser *(Lynbrook, NY)*

> No summer barbeque at our home would ever be complete without my dad's corn salad. It has become a tradition, since it is light, fresh, and a nice compliment to the classic macaroni and potato salad served at most picnics.
>
> *Story by Mary Elizabeth*

4 (17 oz.) cans corn, drained, or 6-8 ears fresh white and yellow corn

½ cup corn oil

2 tablespoons lemon juice, freshly squeezed

¼ cup white vinegar

¼ cup flat-leaf parsley, finely chopped

2 large tomatoes, chopped

1 large green pepper, chopped

1 bunch scallions, finely sliced

¼ teaspoon cayenne pepper

2 teaspoons sea salt

1 teaspoon sugar

½ teaspoon dried basil

Mix all the ingredients in a large bowl. Cover and keep refrigerated until serving. This is best if made a day before serving.

Preparing Fresh Corn

If using fresh corn kernels in your recipe, after you have shucked the corn, stand the cob up straight on a cutting board, cutting kernels off the cob by slicing downward, and rotating the cob until all the kernels are removed. Put them in a large bowl and fill it with water until it gets to 1 inch above the corn. Let it sit for 5 minutes and you will see all the impurities and silk rise to the top; you can skim off with a wire-mesh strainer or a slotted spoon. Repeat the process 3 times until the water begins to run clear.

If the corn is to be served as corn on the cob, the process is different: remove as much of the silk as you can by hand. There are tools designed for this purpose, but an easy trick is to purchase a hard bristle toothbrush to get the fine hairs off. Rinse thoroughly and cook as directed below.

Boil water in a large pot. Turn the heat off, and place 1 cup milk and 1 tablespoon each of sugar and salt into the water. Return to a boil. Place the shucked and clean ears in the water, reduce to a simmer, and continue to cook for 7 minutes. Turn the water off and keep the corn in the water to keep it warm until ready to serve. Following these easy directions will give you perfectly cooked corn every time.

Creamy Cole Slaw

Serves 8

I always make this recipe the morning before I am going to use it so the flavors soak up and the cabbage tastes less pungent. If time allows, it is ideal to make it the night before.

Story by Mary Elizabeth

½ small red onion, chopped (optional)
1 medium head of cabbage, shredded, or 1 (16 oz.) bag cole slaw mix
2 small green peppers, diced
2 medium carrots, shredded
1 cup good-quality mayonnaise
2 tablespoons white vinegar
2 teaspoons sugar
½ teaspoons celery salt
¼ teaspoon celery seed
⅛ teaspoon freshly cracked black pepper
2 tablespoons milk

Combine the first 4 ingredients in a large bowl. In a blender, mix the remaining ingredients and pour over the slaw. Mix thoroughly and chill.

After it is combined, if the cole slaw has too strong of a cabbage flavor, you can add more mayonnaise, one tablespoon at a time, until the desired flavor is achieved.

Sweet Cole Slaw

Jill Patterson *(Lubbock, TX)*
Serves 8

I spend my summers in a small mountain village in Colorado, where a couple, who are about my parents' ages, have "adopted" me—though I am forty. Frequently, they invite me over for meals, which are always made from scratch: no canned goods, no boxed mixes; nothing but the real deal. Each meal in Bob and Bobbie's home is a treat for me: a taste of home and the family rapport that I miss while living twelve hours away from my real family. Each June, on Father's Day, they invite me to join their celebration. As a special salad, Bobbie makes Bob's favorite cole slaw. It is so good that, when I return to the city every year to my university job, I frequently find myself making a big bowl of this salad to take with me to work. It is a nice reminder of my quieter life—my better life in the mountains, and my good friends there. Also, it is so easy to make.

1 (16 oz.) package cole slaw salad mix
3 green apples, peeled and cut into chunks
2 cups pineapple chunks
3 tablespoons mayonnaise
2 tablespoons honey

Mix all the ingredients in a large serving bowl and chill until ready to serve. Once prepared, the salad will stay crisp for two days.

Potato Salad

Marguerite Thoburn Watkins *(Lynchburg, VA)*
Serves 8

What would summertime be without our potato salad? Our church recently had a potato salad dinner cook-off. A doctor's recipe won the most votes, but mine drew compliments, also. I got it from a friend over fifty years ago, when we were all newlyweds. Here it is, as copied from a faded note card.

6 large Idaho potatoes, peeled and cut into ½-inch cubes
1 cup pickle relish or sweet pickles, finely chopped
6 eggs, hard boiled, cooled, and diced
2 cups good-quality mayonnaise
1 medium onion, diced
4 stalks celery, thinly sliced
1 green pepper, diced (optional)
1 dash celery seed
¼ cup sugar
½ teaspoon each salt and freshly ground pepper

Boil a large pot of water. Drop the potatoes in and cook for 20 minutes on high until tender when pierced with a fork (do not overcook). Immediately drain and run cold water over them to stop the cooking process. Set aside and allow them to cool while preparing the dressing.

In a large bowl, mix the all the ingredients (except the potatoes) until well-blended. Toss in the potatoes and stir until each one is well-coated. Cover with plastic wrap and refrigerate until ready to serve.

All-American Macaroni Salad

Elizabeth Meyers *(Port Jefferson Station, NY)*
Serves 6-8

There is nothing like old-fashioned homemade macaroni salad, and my mom makes it the best. With just a few simple ingredients, she transforms simple pasta into a salad that you would expect to find at your local deli counter or restaurant. Look no further: you now have the recipe for your next Fourth of July picnic.

Story by Monica

1 cup mayonnaise
3 tablespoons white vinegar
2 tablespoons prepared dark mustard
1 teaspoon sugar
1 teaspoon sea salt
½ teaspoon pepper
8 ounces macaroni (either elbow, ditalini, or shells), cooked and drained
1 cup celery, sliced
1 cup green or red pepper, chopped
½ cup yellow onion, chopped

In a large bowl, stir together the mayonnaise, vinegar, mustard, sugar, salt, and pepper until smooth. Add the macaroni, celery, pepper, and onion, and then toss to coat well. Cover and chill. Best when refrigerated overnight. Makes 5 cups.

Irene Roarke's Macaroni Salad

Kathy Cromer *(Wantagh, NY)*
Serves 6-8

> I came from a large family. As a child, I can remember frequent backyard barbeques and picnics in the park, where you could always count on everyone bringing their specialty dishes. I particularly remember my aunt Lily's baked beans, aunt Catherine's potato salad, and my mom Irene's macaroni salad. It differed from most because she added tuna. My mom's dish is now the one that I bring to family gatherings. I sometimes will have it as a meal on a warm summer's evening.

1 pound pasta (elbows, bowties, or spirals)
1½- 2 cups good-quality mayonnaise
¼ cup cider vinegar
½ cup milk
2 (6 oz.) cans Italian tuna, packed in olive oil, drained, and flaked
3 hard boil eggs, chopped
1 tablespoon flat-leaf parsley, chopped
2 medium tomatoes, chopped
Sea salt and freshly cracked black pepper to taste

Cook pasta until al dente, drain, and spray with cold water. Set aside. In a separate bowl, blend the mayonnaise, vinegar, and milk. Mix into the pasta. Add tuna and eggs, and toss. Add parsley, salt, and pepper, and mix. Chill. Before serving, mix in extra mayonnaise if needed, and top with chopped tomatoes.

Cucumber Salad

Elizabeth Meyers *(Port Jefferson Station, NY)*
Serves 6

My mom served this refreshing cucumber salad on many summer evenings throughout my childhood. She learned the preparation from my German grandmother, Margaret Reger, who had learned it from her mother. A nice alternative to a green salad, this salad stays fresh in the refrigerator for at least a week, with the flavors getting stronger each day.

Story by Monica

2 medium cucumbers, thinly sliced
⅓ cup cider vinegar
½ cup water
2 tablespoons sugar
½ tablespoon sea salt
⅛ teaspoon pepper
Fresh dill or parsley for garnish

Place your cucumbers into a glass bowl. Mix vinegar, water, sugar, salt, and pepper. Pour over the cucumbers. Cover and refrigerate for at least 3 hours, stirring occasionally. Sprinkle with freshly snipped dill or parsley before serving.

Chilled Cucumber and Pickled Ginger Salad

Chef Christopher Holt, George Martin's Restaurant
(Rockville Centre, NY)
Serves 4-6

2 large cucumbers, very thinly sliced
½ red onion, thinly sliced
2 scallions, thinly sliced
2 tablespoons pickled ginger, chopped
2 tablespoons red or rice wine vinegar
4 tablespoons olive oil
Juice of 1 lime
2 teaspoons sugar
Sea salt and freshly cracked black pepper to taste

Slice the cucumbers, using a mandolin or vegetable slicer. Toss together with onion and scallions. Add pickled ginger, vinegar, oil, lime juice, sugar, salt, and pepper. Chill for 1 hour. Serve over your favorite grilled fish, such as salmon, swordfish, tuna, halibut, or bluefish.

Greek Pasta Salad

Darcy Grainger, Darcy's Delights *(Sayville, NY)*
Serves 8

Salad

1 pound bowtie pasta, cooked

2 medium ripe tomatoes, chopped

1 purple onion, sliced fine

4-5 scallions, diced

½ each green, yellow, and red peppers, chopped

½ pound kalamata olives

½-¾ pounds feta cheese, crumbled

Dressing

½ teaspoon sea salt (optional)

1-1½ teaspoons of freshly cracked black pepper

1-1½ teaspoons garlic powder

1-1½ tablespoons oregano

1 lemon, squeezed thoroughly over salad

¼ cup red wine vinegar

½ cup olive oil

In a large salad bowl, toss the ingredients for dressing thoroughly, and pour over feta cheese. Mix in the salad ingredients and serve.

Summer Salad with Poppy Seed Dressing

Kate Saggio *(Island Park, NY)*
Serves 6-8

1 egg
¾ cup sugar
1 tablespoon dijon mustard
⅔ cup red wine vinegar
1 teaspoon sea salt
3 tablespoons grated onion plus juice (retain the juice that comes from grating the onion)
2 cups vegetable oil
2 tablespoons poppy seeds
1 cup pine nuts, toasted
2 quarts strawberries, sliced
16 ounces mixed salad greens

Blend the first 6 ingredients in a blender, and then add the oil slowly to emulsify. Pour into a bowl, toss with the salad greens, and, just before serving, add the poppy seeds, pine nuts, and strawberries. This recipe makes a quart of dressing, which can be refrigerated for up to a week.

Chef's Tip

Here is another way to "emulsify" (combining ingredients that normally do not mix with the help of a stabilizer such as honey, egg, or mustard). If you prefer not to use your blender, place your ingredients, except the oil, in a metal mixing bowl, and then place the bowl on a damp towel to prevent it from spinning around while you mix. Whisk together vigorously; pour the oil in a slow and steady stream using a spouted measuring cup. Whisk continuously until all the oil has been incorporated and a thick, smooth consistency is achieved. By properly emulsifying your dressing, it will never separate.

Grilled Hearts of Romaine Drizzled with Dijon Vinaigrette

Chef Christopher Holt, George Martin's Restaurant
(Rockville Centre, NY)
Serves 6 as an appetizer or 12 as a side dish

Salad

3 hearts romaine, stems attached

2 tablespoons olive oil

½ cup cooked bacon, chopped

5 ounces crumbled bleu cheese

1½ cups croutons

2 tomatoes, chopped

Sea salt and freshly cracked black pepper to taste

Dijon Vinaigrette

¼ teaspoon dijon mustard

⅛ teaspoon honey

1 teaspoon fresh lemon juice

¼ cup red wine vinegar

¾ cup olive oil

Sea salt and freshly cracked black pepper to taste

Salad

Cut the romaine in half from top to bottom. Rinse gently under running water and allow it to dry for a moment.

Sprinkle each half of the romaine with olive oil, salt, and pepper.

Place the cut (flat-side) down on a hot clean grill for about 1½ minutes, flip for 30 seconds, and transfer to a serving platter.

At this point, you can trim the stem.

Top each half of romaine with vinaigrette, bleu cheese, bacon, croutons, and tomatoes.

You can feel free to change up the toppings on this salad. So many things work well, including ranch dressing, bleu cheese dressing, creamy Italian, Caesar, walnuts, pecans, cucumber, and onion.

Dijon Vinaigrette

Stir together mustard, honey, lemon, and vinegar. Allow to rest 1 minute. Use a whisk to blend in the oil slowly. Season with salt and pepper.

Arugula Salad with Pear and Bleu Cheese

Linda Longo *(Medford, NJ)*
Serves 8

Salad

2 bunches arugula, washed, dried, and rough-chopped
1 head Bibb lettuce, rough-chopped
Juice ½ lemon
1 ripe pear, sliced thinly
8 ounces bleu cheese, crumbled
½ cup dried cranberries (optional)

Dressing

1 shallot, minced
2 tablespoons white wine vinegar
¼ cup apricot jam or all-fruit spread
⅓ cup extra virgin olive oil

Salad

Toss all the ingredients in a large bowl.

Dressing

Emulsify (see Chef's Tip, page 52) all the ingredients. Pour over the salad just before serving.

Mesclun and Red-Leaf Lettuce Salad

Chef Geraldine Pollack *(Islip, NY)*

Dressing

Juice of 2 lemons
1 tablespoon shallots, chopped
½ cup extra virgin olive oil
Sea salt and freshly cracked black pepper to taste

Salad

6 ounces mesclun
6 ounces red-leaf lettuce
4 ounces artichoke, grilled and chopped
8 asparagus, grilled and trimmed
2 Portobello mushrooms, grilled and cut in strips
3 ounces provolone, shaved

Dressing

Combine lemon juice and shallots in a bowl and slowly incorporate olive oil. Adjust seasoning with salt and pepper. Set aside.

Salad

Combine greens with grilled asparagus and mushrooms, and toss gently with dressing.
Place on a serving platter and top with provolone; serve immediately.

Strawberry Fig Basil Salad

Nancy Curry and Catherine Pepe, Temecula Olive Oil Company
(Temecula, CA)
Serves 4

This is a recipe from one of our customers. With the huge annual strawberry harvest, this is another great way to use those luscious fruits.

1 shallot, finely diced
2 tablespoons Temecula Olive Oil Company Vanilla & Fig Balsamic Vinegar (or sherry vinegar)
4 ripe black mission figs
½ cup Temecula Olive Oil Company Fresh Basil Olive Oil
2 handfuls fresh arugula, roughly chopped
¼ cup fresh flat-leaf parsley, chopped
½ cup fresh mint leaves, chopped
1 handful young, tender frisee, roughly chopped
1 cup fresh strawberries, sliced
2 ounces goat cheese, chilled
Sea salt and freshly cracked black pepper to taste

Combine shallot and vinegar in a small bowl with salt and pepper. Let stand for 10-15 minutes. Trim fig stems, removing anything fibrous, but preserving the tear-drop shape. Cut into quarters lengthwise, and set aside. Whisk olive oil into the vinegar and shallot mixture. Combine the greens and herbs, and gently toss with just enough vinaigrette to lightly coat. Place the greens on a serving platter, and nestle the fig quarters and strawberries around the greens. Crumble the goat cheese on top. Drizzle any remaining vinaigrette over the fruit and cheese, and serve immediately.

Zesty Orange and Cucumber Salad

Nancy Curry and Catherine Pepe, Temecula Olive Oil Company
(Temecula, CA)

2 cucumbers, peeled, seeded, and thinly sliced
5 large oranges, peeled and sectioned
¼ cup red onion, thinly sliced
2 tablespoons lime juice, freshly squeezed
2 teaspoons sea salt
2 teaspoons paprika
1 small head iceberg lettuce, chopped into 1-inch pieces
3 tablespoons Temecula Olive Oil Company Picante Pepper Olive Oil

Combine the first 6 ingredients and toss gently. Cover and chill at least 1 hour. Pour the mixture over the lettuce in a large bowl, and toss gently with olive oil. Serve immediately.

Green Beans with Mustard and Shallot Vinaigrette

Serves 8

2 shallots, minced
2 tablespoons dijon mustard
2 tablespoons balsamic vinegar
½ cup olive oil
2 pounds fresh green beans, steamed
¼ cup fresh dill, chopped
Sea salt and freshly cracked black pepper to taste

Blanch and shock green beans as described below.

Place shallots, mustard, vinegar, salt, and pepper in a small bowl, and while whisking, slowly drizzle in olive oil, creating an emulsion (see Chef's Tip on page 52). Toss the green beans with the dressing to coat. Quickly add dill and toss to combine. Serve at room temperature.

Chef's Tip

Blanching and shocking your vegetables will make them remain crisp and bright green. Fill a large pot of water with salt (making it salty enough to taste like sea water) and an ice bath (a large bowl full of ice and water).

Place green beans into the boiling water. Test the vegetables for doneness; green beans should be crisp, yet cooked (about 2-4 minutes). Using a slotted spoon, quickly remove them from the boiling water, and plunge them into the ice bath to shock them. This abruptly halts the cooking process.

Allow them to cool completely and drain.

Elegant Watermelon Salad

A Silverware Affair *(Chattanooga,TN)*

½ red onion, thinly sliced
Juice of 1 lime
1 whole watermelon, seeds removed and fruit cubed
4 ounces goat cheese, diced (may put in freezer for 15 minutes
prior to ease slicing)
4 ounces dried figs (fresh figs can be used, too, if desired)
¼ cup fresh mint

Mix onions in lime juice to reduce the strength of the taste. After 10
minutes, combine all the ingredients, toss lightly, and serve.

Gazpacho

Nancy Curry and Catherine Pepe, Temecula Olive Oil Company
(Temecula, CA)

1 large green pepper
1 large cucumber
1 large onion
3-4 garlic cloves
½ cup fresh parsley, chopped
1 pound crushed tomatoes
½ cup bread crumbs
¼ cup Temecula Olive Oil Company Frantoio Olive Oil
¼ cup red wine vinegar
2 (5½ oz.).cans tomato juice
1 ripe avocado, sliced thinly lengthwise
Sea salt, freshly cracked black pepper, lemon juice, and hot sauce to taste

Take the seeds and ribs out of the pepper, and remove the seeds from the cucumber. Chop the fresh vegetables to a chunky stage, and set a third aside for later use. Mix the remaining veggies, tomatoes, bread crumbs, olive oil, vinegar, and half the tomato juice in a blender or food processor until pureed. Add the chunky vegetables and seasonings (salt, cracked pepper, lemon juice, and hot sauce) to taste. Refrigerate. Serve ice cold. Garnish with chopped avocado.

North Fork Clam Chowder

Chef Mike Farrell, North Fork Country Club *(Cutchogue, NY)*
Serves 12

1 dozen cherrystone clams or small chowders
1 cup dry white wine
6 slices bacon, diced
1 tablespoon olive oil
1 onion, peeled, diced
1 clove garlic, chopped
2 carrots, peeled and diced
1 parsnip, peeled and diced
4 ribs celery, diced
½ red or green pepper, cored, seeded, and diced
2 ears corn, husked, fibers cleaned off, kernels removed from cob, and cob reserved

1 cup chopped tomato or 1 (14.5 oz.) can peeled tomato, diced with juice
4 cups water or clam juice
3 medium red potatoes, peeled and diced
2½ tablespoons kosher salt
½ teaspoon freshly cracked black pepper
1 bay leaf
1 tablespoon fresh oregano, chopped, or ½ teaspoon dried
1 tablespoon fresh thyme, chopped, or ½ teaspoon dried
3 tablespoons flour

Place clams in a large stock-pot with white wine and enough water to cover. Steam until the clams open, and drain the reserving broth. Remove the clams from their shells when cool enough to handle, chop, and reserve.

In the stock-pot, render the diced bacon in olive oil, and cook until lightly browned, stirring. Pour off all but 1 tablespoon of bacon fat, and reserve.

Sauté onions and garlic in with the bacon until translucent. Add the rest of the vegetables, and sauté until soft. Add the reserved clam broth, tomatoes, clams, and water or juice. Add the reserved corn cob, and bring to a boil, skimming, and then adding red potatoes, salt, pepper, and herbs. Add flour to the reserved bacon fat and stir to form a paste; add to the pot. Stir into the soup, and bring to a boil, reducing and simmering for 30 minutes or so until the potato is soft.

Seafood Bisque

Chef Richard Larkin, Snapper Inn *(Oakdale, NY)*
Serves 20

Fish Stock
Fish bones
Shrimp and lobster shells, if available
3 carrots, rough-chopped
2 stalks celery, rough-chopped
4 onions, rough-chopped
1 lemon, split
½ handful peppercorns (approximately 1 tablespoon)
3-4 bay leaves
1 bunch each thyme, chives, and parsley

Bisque
2 bottles sherry wine
7 quarts heavy cream
1 lobster base
Tomato juice to color
Roux to thicken (see Chef's Tips)
Old Bay seasoning to taste

Fish Stock
Add all the ingredients in a large stock-pot, simmering for approximately 3 hours, and strain.

Bisque
Burn off the sherry, adding the cream and base. Add fish stock and tomato juice until orange-pink in color. Bring to a boil, adding roux until thickened, and strain. Then add the Old Bay seasonings to taste.

Shrimp and Pasta Salad

Serves 12-20

Every Fourth of July, I go to the annual parade in Southampton, NY, complete with floats, marching bands, celebrity impersonators, and even a float of a burning building to show the firefighting prowess of the local fire department, which promptly puts it out. My cousin Patty and her husband Mickey run out to Main Street at around 6 o'clock that morning to find a prime spot to set up tables, chairs, blankets, coolers, and umbrellas. Most of the family shows up just in time for the parade, and we sit down like royalty to enjoy the festivities. Afterward, we each grab something to carry and tote it all back to their house for an old-fashioned barbeque on their front lawn. Their porch—and pretty much the whole town—is decorated with Americana. We all contribute a dish. My aunt loves shrimp, so I came up with this macaroni salad for her.

Story by Monica

1 pound shaped pasta, cooked (lobsters, wagon wheels, etc.)
1 (8 oz.) bottle Italian dressing, divided
3 stalks celery, diced
3 scallions, sliced (greens included)
1 large red pepper, diced
1 cup grape tomatoes, sliced
1½ pounds medium to large shrimp, cooked and tails removed
3-5 tablespoons mayonnaise
1-3 tablespoons Old Bay seasoning
Sea salt to taste (optional)

In a large bowl, mix pasta, ½ bottle of Italian dressing, celery, scallions, pepper, and tomatoes. In a separate bowl, mix shrimp with the remaining Italian dressing. Cover both bowls with plastic wrap and place in the refrigerator to marinate overnight. In the morning, stir together the pasta and the shrimp mixes with their marinades. Add the mayonnaise, Old Bay, and salt, and then mix. Serve chilled.

Italian Pasta Salad

Elizabeth Meyers *(Port Jefferson Station, NY)*
Serves 12-20

> To the family's delight, my mom makes this very colorful Italian pasta salad for our summer parties even though she doesn't eat the meats in it, meticulously picking them off her plate. My cousin Joanie's boyfriend, Tommy, makes a similar version and these days we switch off between his and my mom's. Tommy graciously makes a special bowl, sans meat, just for my mom.
>
> *Story by Monica*

Salad

1 pound cooked pasta (tri-colored rotelli, but any pasta will do)
1 pound pepperoni, cubed
½ pound salami or boiled ham, cubed
1 pound provolone cheese, cubed
3 stalks celery, diced
2 carrots, cut diagonally into ¼-inch pieces
1 (15 oz.) can black olives, sliced
1 (12 oz.) can green olives, sliced
1 pint cherry or grape tomatoes
1 large green pepper, diced
1 small yellow onion, diced
1 head fresh broccoli, florets only, blanched

Dressing

½ cup white vinegar
¾ cups extra virgin olive oil
1 tablespoon fresh oregano, chopped

Season to taste with:

Sea salt (about 1 teaspoon)
Freshly cracked black pepper (about ½ teaspoon)
Garlic powder (about 1 tablespoon)
Chopped parsley (about 1 tablespoon)
Emeril's Essence (about 1 teaspoon)

Salad

Toss all the ingredients in a large bowl, except the pasta.

Dressing

Mix all the ingredients of the dressing. Add to the pasta just after cooking and toss. Mix in the rest of the ingredients and refrigerate for several hours; stir right before serving.

Mediterranean Wrap

Susan Prior *(Rising Sun, MD)*
Serves 4

¾ cup tomato, chopped
1 tablespoon purple onion, diced
1 tablespoon fresh cilantro, chopped
1 teaspoon lime juice
⅛ teaspoon sea salt
1 clove garlic, minced
1 cup long-grain rice, cooked
2 teaspoon basil
1 cup sweet red pepper, chopped
¾ cup zucchini, diced
¾ cup yellow squash, diced
¼ cup purple onion, diced
2 tablespoons balsamic vinegar
2 teaspoons olive oil
4 (8-inch) tortillas
¼ cup feta cheese, crumbled

Combine first 6 ingredients in a bowl; set tomato mixture aside. Combine rice and basil; set aside.

Arrange sweet red pepper, zucchini, yellow squash, and onion in a single layer on a baking sheet.

Broil for 12 minutes or until vegetables are browned, then spoon into a large bowl. Drizzle

vinegar and olive oil over vegetables, and toss to coat. Warm tortillas according to

package directions. Spoon ¼ cup of the rice mixture down the center of each tortilla. Top each

serving with ½ cup of the roasted vegetables, 2 tablespoons of the tomato mixture, and 1 tablespoon of feta cheese; roll up.

Southwestern Stew

Lou De Santis *(Eastport, NY)*
Serves 6

At sixty-two, I decided to retire and learn how to cook. I always loved doing it, but never knew how, so, I entered culinary school. Here is a recipe from my days in the military at Davis Monthan Air Force Base in Tucson, AZ, which we brought over from Vietnam. The bottle of beer was added to the recipe in Nam, when we were running for our lives from form incoming artillery, and a solider had to get rid of the bottle of beer that he was holding and just dumped it into the pot. It worked out pretty well.

3 pounds lizard meat (or stew
meat: veal or beef)
Flour, to coat meat
⅓ cup olive oil
2 large onions, diced
2 cloves garlic, diced
1 tablespoon olive oil
12 ounces beer
3 cups beef broth
1 teaspoon oregano

2 large jalapeño peppers, diced
½ cup diced sun-dried tomatoes
(soaked first in water to soften)
3 small zucchini, peeled and
diced
1 (20 oz.) can chick peas
1 (6 oz.) can black olives
Sea salt and freshly cracked
black pepper to taste
1 pound cooked egg noodles

Cube the meat into bite-size pieces. Flour the meat and brown it in olive oil. Remove from the pan and put aside. Add a tablespoon of olive oil, and brown the onions and garlic. Put aside. Now, turn the heat up on the pan, and deglaze by pouring in the beer, stirring and scraping the bottom of the pot until all the pieces of browned meat and flour are combined. Let the beer boil down to about 6 ounces.

Lower the heat, add the beef stock, oregano, meat, and onion, and simmer for 1 hour. Add jalapeños and sun-dried tomatoes, and simmer for another ½ hour. Add zucchini, chick peas, and olives. Cook until the zucchini is tender. Add salt and pepper to taste.

Serve over noodles.

Roasted Tomato and Shallot Marmalade

Chef Therese Harding, The Classic Catering People
(Owings Mills, MD)
Yields 1 jar

1 cup plum tomatoes, diced and seeded
3 tablespoons olive oil, divided
1 teaspoon brown sugar
1 cup shallots, diced
1 tablespoon balsamic syrup (see recipe below)
Sea salt and freshly cracked black pepper to taste

Preheat an oven to 310°F.

In a small bowl, toss plum tomatoes with 2 tablespoons of olive oil and brown sugar.

In a separate small bowl, toss shallots with the remaining 1 tablespoon of olive oil.

On a sheet pan, slowly roast the tomatoes for 40 minutes. On a separate sheet pan, slowly roast the shallots for 30 minutes. The vegetables should be translucent when finished.

Cool the vegetables to room temperature. Add 1 tablespoon of balsamic syrup to shallots.

Combine the shallots and tomatoes; season with salt and pepper.

Balsamic Syrup

Makes ⅓ cup

1 cup balsamic vinegar

Pour vinegar into a small, heavy, non-reactive saucepan. Bring to a boil over high heat; reduce by ⅓ (about 14 minutes). Cool in the pan. Pour into a small glass jar, cover, and store at room temperature.

Part III

APPETIZERS AND BEVERAGES

APPETIZERS AND BEVERAGES

With a taste of this and a bit of that, it is always a treat to nibble something new before a big barbeque. Asking your guests to bring an appetizer to your get together is pretty much a given these days, and offers a great opportunity to try an assortment of tasty treats from all walks of life. The gardener in your group may bring bruschetta with fresh basil or cheese-stuffed jalapeño peppers; the fisherman may bring shrimp; and the mom will bring chicken fingers.

Monica likes to send her son Matt out to the garden to pick cherry tomatoes and herbs while she busily prepares her appetizers. He always comes back into the kitchen amazed and delighted by the plentiful harvest that he discovers every summer. His knowledge of cooking is enhanced, as is his enthusiasm for matching up the correct herbs with each dish. He is also empowered to prepare more dishes on his own while away at school—yet another way of passing on the family's love of cooking to the next generation. Mary Elizabeth's daughter Nicole's interest in cooking was initially nurtured at home, and was taken to another level when she became a chef.

Summer appetizers differ quite a bit from the heavier ones served at other times of the year. Fresh fruit on skewers is a regular feature at Monica's barbeques, and both kids and adults reach for it first (in fact, it is usually the first food to be finished). Clams on the Half-Shell (page 73) are another favorite at family gatherings at Monica's brother-in-law Tim's house. He expertly opens dozens of raw clams as his guests hover around him, their mouths watering for a taste of the juicy morsels. Steamers and mussels marinara are another delicious choice, as are fresh vegetable platters with several zesty dips or cool Gazpacho (page 60) that satisfies the palate while keeping it light.

Lemonade using freshly squeezed lemons and homemade ginger ale with grated ginger are so refreshing on a hot day. Make sun tea in the morning and let it steep throughout the day until your guests arrive. You can also try freezing raspberries, nasturtiums, or mint leaves in your ice cube tray, and use them to make colorful and yummy drinks.

With drinks in hand and appetites whetted, you are ready for the main event, and your guests will be anxious to try their next course. Is there a better way to spend a summer day than sharing good food and good times with friends and family?

Clams on the Half-Shell

Serves 4-8

4 dozen clams
2 cups water
½ large onion, sliced
2½ sprigs of parsley
2½ tablespoons fresh lemon juice
Unsalted butter for dipping
Sea salt to taste

Cleansing Brine
½ cup sea salt
1½ gallons water
Wire brush

Keep your clams refrigerated or on ice until ready to use. First, clean the clams by making a brine using ½ cup of sea salt (or any non-iodized salt) to 1½ gallons of water, discarding any clams where the shell seal is broken or are open before steaming. Soak for about 15 minutes to release any grit on the outside of the clam. Strain the brine water and run cold water over the clams in a strainer for a couple of minutes, while scrubbing clean with a wire brush. Rub gently with a towel to clean off any remaining sand or grit.

In a large steamer pot, place your clams, water, onion, parsley, and lemon juice. Steam for about 5-10 minutes or until the shells open. Discard any clams where the shell has not opened. Serve in a large bowl nestled in the strained steaming broth with clarified butter and sliced lemons on the side. Place another bowl on the table for the discarded shells.

How to open clams to be on the half-shell? It takes a brave soul to take on the arduous task of opening fresh clams. Start with cold clams that have been refrigerated or kept cold on ice. Clean as indicated above. Using a special clam knife (one with a blunt or rounded point; the blade shorter than, but as dull as, a butter knife), hold the clam in one hand, the knife in the other, so it is parallel to the clamshell opening. With the blade as close to the top of the clamshell as possible, cut into the clam. You may have to wiggle and wedge into larger clams, working from one side of the clam seam to the other, pushing far into the clam to cut the muscle that is holding it closed. Rotate your knife back and forth until the shell is finally open. Once opened, twist off the top shell, and then separate the clam from the remaining muscle under the meat, leaving the clam nestled in its own juice on the bottom of the shell. Serve with cocktail sauce and lemon juice. Keep a bowl handy to capture any juice that drips out while opening. For use in chowder or dips, cut out the whole clam and place with the clam juice in your catch bowl, then following your recipe for chowder or dip.

Mexican Shrimp Cocktail

A Silverware Affaire *(Chattanooga, TN)*
Serves 2

Shrimp

10 large gulf shrimp, peeled and deveined
1 tablespoon extra virgin olive oil
1 teaspoon garlic salt
Juice from ½ lime
Freshly cracked black pepper to taste

Cocktail Sauce

1 avocado, diced
½ red onion, diced
1 whole red tomato, diced
1 whole jalapeño, diced
¼ red bell pepper, diced
¼ cup fresh cilantro, chopped
¼ cup kernel corn
Juice of ½ lime
8 ounces organic tortilla chips
Sea salt and freshly cracked black pepper to taste

Shrimp

Sauté shrimp in olive oil with garlic salt, pepper, and lime until pink and cooked through (approximately 5 minutes).

Cocktail Sauce

Mix the above ingredients lightly and place in martini glasses. Garnish with shrimp and tortilla chips. For a different spin on this recipe, see the next recipe.

Tuscan Summer Shrimp Cocktail

A Silverware Affaire *(Chattanooga, TN)*

Shrimp

10 large gulf shrimp, peeled and deveined
1 tablespoon extra virgin olive oil
1 teaspoon garlic salt
Juice of ½ lemon
Freshly cracked black pepper to taste

Crostinis

4 tablespoons extra virgin olive oil
2 cloves garlic, minced
1 loaf baguette bread, cut into thin slices

Cocktail Sauce

½ red onion, diced
1 whole tomato, diced
¼ cup fresh basil, cut into ribbons
½ cup fresh mozzarella, diced
1 tablespoon extra virgin olive oil
1 tablespoon balsamic vinegar
1 teaspoon sugar
Sea salt and freshly cracked black pepper to taste

Shrimp

Sauté shrimp in olive oil with garlic salt, pepper, and lemon until pink and cooked through (approximately 5 minutes).

Crostinis

Mix olive oil and garlic. Brush slices of the baguettes with the olive oil mixture. Toast in the oven until lightly brown (approximately 5 minutes at 375°F). Set aside.

Cocktail Sauce

Mix the above ingredients lightly and place in martini glasses. Garnish with shrimp and crostinis, topping each glass with several ribbons of basil.

Chef's Tip

Ribbon-cut basil is easily prepared by using a technique called chiffonade. Here is how it is done: Wash and dry the basil thoroughly, and then stack the leaves in the same direction on a clean cutting board. Roll the leaves lengthwise. With a good knife, start to thinly slice the basil and ribbon-shaped strips will start to appear.

Grilled Basil Shrimp

Nancy Curry and Catherine Pepe, Temecula Olive Oil Company
(Temecula, CA)
Serves 4-6

2½ tablespoons Temecula Olive Oil Company Fresh Basil Olive Oil
¼ cup butter, melted
Juice of 1½ lemons
3 tablespoons brown mustard
½ cup minced fresh basil
3 cloves garlic, minced
3 pounds fresh shrimp, peeled and deveined
Sea salt and freshly cracked white pepper to taste

In a shallow, non-porous dish or bowl, mix together olive oil and butter. Stir in lemon juice, mustard, basil, and garlic, season with salt and pepper. Add shrimp, and toss to coat. Cover and refrigerate for 1 hour. Preheat a grill to high heat. Remove shrimp from the marinade and thread onto skewers. Discard the marinade. Lightly oil the grill grate, and arrange the skewers on the preheated grill. Cook for 4 minutes, turning once or until opaque.

Before getting started, soak wooden skewers in water for 20 minutes to avoid burning on your grill.

Fire-Roasted Mussels with Citrus Garlic Butter or Fresh Tomato Salsa

Chef Christopher Holt, George Martin's Restaurant
(Rockville Centre, NY)
Serves 4

Mussels
3 pounds farm-raised mussels (preferably Prince Edward Island), cleaned with beards removed
3 tablespoons olive oil
1 teaspoon kosher salt
¼ teaspoons freshly cracked black pepper

Fresh Tomato Salsa
3 medium ripe tomatoes, chopped
½ small red onion, chopped
6 leaves cilantro, chopped
Juice of 1 lime
2 teaspoons red wine vinegar
6 teaspoons olive oil
Dash of Tabasco or hot sauce
Sea salt and freshly cracked black pepper to taste

Citrus Garlic Butter
½ pound butter
4 cloves garlic, cut in half
Zest of 1 lemon (see note below)
Zest of 1 orange (see note below)
2 teaspoons fresh parsley, chopped

Mussels

Discard any mussels that are open or have broken shells. Gently toss the mussels with the olive oil, salt, and pepper. Chill the mussels until ready to grill.

On a hot, clean grill, gently place the mussels, and cover with the grill lid (if your grill does not have a lid, cover the mussels with a large metal bowl).

Cook for 2 minutes, and as the mussels pop open, remove them from the grill and place in a large bowl, so, you can toss them with your choice of sauce.

Fresh Tomato Salsa

Chop the tomatoes, red onion, and cilantro by hand or simply pulse in your food processor. Add the lime, vinegar, oil, hot sauce, salt, and pepper. Stir well and let it rest for 1 hour before adding to your mussels. Serve this version of the mussels with a clean, crisp pilsner beer.

Citrus Garlic Butter

In a small saucepan, gently melt the butter with the garlic over a low heat.

Allow the butter and garlic to cook together for 3 minutes.

Remove from the heat and allow to rest for 1 minute. Remove the cloves of garlic from the butter, and add the zest and parsley. Toss with the hot mussels. Serve with a light white wine.

Reserve the zested lemon and orange, and cut into wedges to garnish the mussels.

Lime Chicken Fingers

Nancy Curry and Catherine Pepe, Temecula Olive Oil Company
(Temecula, CA)
Serves 4-6

2 pounds boneless, skinless chicken tenders
⅓ cup Temecula Olive Oil Company Fajita Frenzy Olive Oil
4 cloves garlic, minced
3 tablespoons fresh cilantro, chopped
Sea salt and freshly cracked black pepper to taste

Trim the fat from the chicken tenders. Place between sheets of waxed paper and pound with a rolling pin to flatten. Combine all the other ingredients (except the salt and pepper) and marinate for about 20 minutes to an hour. Remove from the marinade. Sprinkle chicken with salt and pepper. Grill for 2 minutes on each side.

Basic Chicken Wings

Dee Fitzgerald *(Lake Forest, CA)*
Serves 4-6

> While doing research for my book *Harnessing a Heritage*, I learned how closely foods are tied with cultures. One recipe that works well with introducing children to food and culture is adapting a basic chicken wings recipe to fit their heritage (see the box below for some ideas). The process lends itself to involvement with even very young children, and the finished product is guaranteed to become a favorite. The varieties are limitless. The important factor is the involvement and learning about the foods of one's culture.

1 pound chicken wings (wings, drumettes, or mixed) or chicken strips
4 tablespoons herbs and spices, as desired
1 cup bread crumbs
¼ cup oil

Rinse the chicken wings and pat dry. Mix herbs and bread crumbs, and place in a paper or plastic bag. Dip the wings in oil and place in a bag with seasoned bread crumbs. Shake the bag until the wings are coated. Remove from the bag and place on a non-stick, foiled cookie sheet. Bake at 350°F for 45 minutes, turning once.

Dipping Sauce Variations

- Buffalo wings, from Buffalo, NY, are a popular choice, and can be made in various degrees of hotness. The sauce is not so much a dipping sauce as a covering on the wings. This can be used instead of the bread crumbs, but works equally well as a coating for the above recipe. The wings would be coated with oil that has been seasoned with garlic, chili oil, and Tabasco to taste. Cooked wings can be sautéed with the sauce. The traditional dipping sauce is ranch or bleu cheese dressing. Celery stalks are also a common accompaniment.

- An Asian variation is to add chili oil to the oil in which you dip the wings in the basic recipe. You can control the hotness by the amount of chili oil used. Popular dipping sauces would include teriyaki and plum sauce. You can vary the bread crumbs by using panko (Japanese bread crumbs) and spices such as five-spice powder.

- A Filipino twist is to use sweet chili sauce as a dip. Chinese mustard sauce (from dry mustard or commercial) also works.

- Indian cultures might use tikka sauce instead of oil and use a curry-based dipping sauce.

- Italians may prefer using Parmesan cheese as a seasoning instead of bread crumbs and marinara sauce as a dip.

- Mexicans could use cilantro as an herb and salsa as the dipping sauce.

Rosemary Shortbread Cookies

Nancy Curry and Catherine Pepe, Temecula Olive Oil Company
(Temecula, CA)
Serves 6

> This shortbread features Temecula Olive Oil Company's non-traditional flavored oil. The fresh rosemary taste is created by crushing the olives along with the herb, and then using it for grilled meats and veggies, pastas, and breads. You can also use a splash when making a vinaigrette.

1¼ cups unsalted butter, softened
⅔ cup white sugar
2 tablespoons fresh Temecula Olive Oil Company Rosemary Olive Oil (see note below)
2¾ cups all-purpose flour
¼ teaspoon sea salt
2 teaspoons white sugar, for decorating

In a medium bowl, cream together the butter, fresh rosemary olive oil, and white sugar until light and fluffy. Stir in the flour and salt until well-blended. The dough will be somewhat soft. Cover and refrigerate for 1 hour. Preheat the oven to 375°F. Line cookie sheets with parchment paper. On a lightly floured surface, roll the dough out to ¼-inch thickness. Cut into 1½- by 2-inch rectangles. Place cookies 1 inch apart on the lined cookie sheets. Sprinkle the raw sugar over the tops. Bake for 8 minutes in the preheated oven or until golden at the edges. Cool on wire racks, and store in an airtight container at room temperature.

Can substitute with Temecula Olive Oil Company D'Luscious Lemon Oil in this recipe for a different flavor.

Clam Dip

Gretel Carlin *(Stony Brook, NY)*
Serves 6-8

My sister-in-law Gretel loves to give parties every season, and she always puts out an appetizing array of dips, crudités, and tapas. She offers something new at each get-together, combined with her guests' favorites, including this clam dip (which is my personal favorite). It takes virtually minutes to prepare using canned or frozen clams; a bit longer if you are opening fresh clams for the dip. Whichever you choose, this dip will always be a hit.

Story by Monica

4 cups minced clams and juice
1 tablespoon lemon juice
½ pound butter
1-2 onions, chopped
Dash Tabasco or any hot sauce
6 cloves garlic, minced
2 tablespoons dried parsley (or equivalent fresh, chopped fine)
2 tablespoons dried oregano (or equivalent fresh, chopped fine)
1-2 cups flavored bread crumbs
4-6 slices of thinly sliced American or cheddar cheese
Sea salt to taste (only if using fresh clams)
1 (9.5 oz.) box crackers or 1 (11.5 oz.) bag tortilla chips

Simmer clams and juice with lemon juice. In another pan, sauté all the ingredients but the bread crumbs. Mix all together, adding bread crumbs. Pour into an 8- by 8-inch baking dish. Cover with slices of cheese and bake at 350°F for 25 minutes. Serve with a cocktail spoon and crackers or tortilla chips.

Fairway Market's Crab Cakes with Tartar Sauce

Danny Glickberg and Chef Mitchel London *(New York, NY)*
Serves 4

Crab Cakes

1 pound jumbo lump crab meat
3 egg yolks
2 tablespoons mustard
4 tablespoons mayonnaise
2 pinches cayenne pepper
½ bunch parsley, chopped
3 scallions, minced
¼ cup bread crumbs
1 tablespoon corn oil

Tartar Sauce

2 cups mayonnaise
6 tablespoons cornichons, sliced, or regular gherkins (not sweet)
3 tablespoons capers
1 tablespoon chives, chopped
½ teaspoon cayenne pepper
Juice of ½ lemon

Crab Cakes

Go through the crab meat to remove the shells, if any. Mix the 3 egg yolks with the mustard, mayonnaise, and cayenne pepper. Gently blend the mayonnaise mixture with the crab meat. Add the parsley and scallions. Dust with as few bread crumbs as you need just to hold the crab cake together.

Heat a heavy pan on top of a stove with 1 tablespoon of corn oil to a medium heat.

Place the crab cake in the pan, and gently brown on one side. Then flip and place in the oven at 375°F for 15 minutes.

Tartar Sauce

Mix all the ingredients together and refrigerate.

Salsa

Serves 6-8

> Like a gallon of milk and loaf of bread, salsa and tortilla chips
> have become a staple in our home. About a year ago, I started to
> eliminate foods with additives and, instead, added organic food
> to my diet whenever possible. So, I decided to make my own
> salsa. Once you have had fresh salsa and you see how easy it is
> to make, you will never go back.
>
> *Story by Mary Elizabeth*

50 grape tomatoes, chopped, or 4 (14.5 oz.) cans petite
diced tomatoes, well-drained
1 bunch fresh cilantro, chopped
1 onion, chopped
1 cup fresh lime juice
1 teaspoon each sea salt and freshly cracked black pepper
6 jalapeño rings, diced (optional)

Mix all the ingredients in a large bowl, cover, and chill before serving.

Guacamole

Serves 6-8

1 tablespoon sea salt
1 cup red onion, chopped
2 tablespoons jalapeños, seeded and chopped
3 tablespoons fresh cilantro leaves, chopped
6 ripe avocados, chopped
¾ cup fresh tomatoes, seeded, chopped, and drained
Fresh lime juice to taste

Mix all the ingredients in a large bowl, cover, and chill before serving.

Chef's Tip

Guacamole is best served fresh, but if you have some leftovers and want to prevent the guacamole from browning, splash lemon juice evenly on top. Cover tightly with plastic wrap. The trick is to press the plastic wrap down against the surface.

Mozzarella, Tomato, and Red Onion Platter with Basil Drizzle

Serves 6-8

The buffet table that I set up in my backyard for family gatherings would not be complete without this dish. Large beef-steak tomatoes flourish on farm stands in the summers on Long Island, alongside bouquets of fresh basil. Most people serve this dish with a balsamic drizzle, but once my friend Chris shared his tangy dressing with me, there was no going back.

Story by Mary Elizabeth

Salad Platter

2 large beef-steak tomatoes, thinly sliced
1 (16 oz.) ball fresh mozzarella, thinly sliced
1 large red onion, thinly sliced

Dressing

½ cup good-quality mayonnaise
3 tablespoons white vinegar
2 tablespoons extra virgin olive oil
2 tablespoons whole milk
1 teaspoon sugar
½ teaspoon sea salt
15 fresh basil leaves

Place all the dressing ingredients in a food processor and blend. Assemble the platter by alternately arranging tomatoes, red onions, and mozzarella. Immediately before serving, drizzle sauce over the platter.

Bruschetta

Serves 4-8

With so much fresh basil and plum and cherry tomatoes in my garden, a day does not go by that bruschetta is not served at our table. It is great for a snack, lunch, or appetizer before dinner. You can purchase premade toast rounds in your grocery store or make them yourself in your oven.

Story by Monica

Topping

8 plum tomatoes, skinned and diced or 24 cherry tomatoes, diced
1 clove garlic, crushed
1 tablespoon extra virgin olive oil
1 teaspoon balsamic vinegar
12-16 basil leaves, finely chopped
1 pound fresh mozzarella cheese, sliced thin

Toasted Rounds of Bread

1 large loaf of either Italian bread or French baguette
$^{1}/_{4}$ cup extra virgin olive oil
Sea salt and freshly ground green peppercorns to taste

Mix together tomatoes, garlic, olive oil, balsamic vinegar, and basil leaves, and set aside. Slice the mozzarella cheese into extra thin, round slices, and set aside. Cut your bread into the thin slices and brush with olive oil on one side. Place face down on a baking sheet, and then place in a preheated 450°F oven for about 5 minutes or until they brown slightly. Take out, turn over, and salt and pepper the olive-oil side. Place the mozzarella on each slice of bread, and top with the tomato-basil mixture. Serve immediately. Extra ingredients can be refrigerated for future use, but there are rarely leftovers.

Caribbean Cooler

Serves 4

4 ounces cream of coconut
4 ounces orange juice, freshly squeezed
16 ounces pineapple juice
8 ounces rum
Nutmeg for garnish

Place all the ingredients in a blender and mix until frothy. Pour over a glass filled with ice. Top with a sprinkle of nutmeg.

Summer Punch

Serves 10-12

2 (2 liter) bottles lemon-lime soda
1 (750 ml.) bottle pink champagne
1 pint pink sherbet (any flavor)
8 ounces frozen strawberries

Mix and serve chilled.

Homemade Ginger Ale

Serves 8

I prefer plain seltzer, which is salt and sugar free, yet still refreshing and bubbly, to flavored sodas: a throw-back to when the seltzer man used to deliver a dozen beautiful blue seltzer bottles right to your front door; a trend that had a grand resurgence when I lived in Park Slope (which then stopped abruptly when no one was returning the bottles back to the company, because they were so pretty and collectable). On the occasion when my sweet tooth acts up, I make my own sodas using fresh ingredients like ginger or lemon. Storin

Story by Monica

2 quart bottles unflavored seltzer
1 (8-inch piece) ginger, frozen, skinned, and finely grated
8 teaspoons stevia to taste
Juice of ¼ lemon

Fill a pitcher(s) with seltzer, adding 1 inch per serving of grated ginger, stevia, and lemon juice. Stir well and pour into glasses with ice. The ginger will gravitate to the bottom of the pitcher; stir before each serving. Serve immediately.

Minty Mojitos

Serves 8

Mojitos are delightfully sugary, minty, tropical concoctions that are easy to make at home, using mint fresh from your garden. I have some friends who only grow mint for this purpose. They are a beautiful drink, served in tall glasses with swirling lime slices and extra mint as garnish.

Story by Monica

8 teaspoons of powdered sugar or stevia (sweeten to taste)
2-4 tablespoons hot water
2 quarts unsweetened seltzer
2-4 limes, sliced in rounds
16 mint leaves for the drink and extra for each glass
8 ounces white rum
Crushed ice

Mix hot water and sugar or stevia until dissolved and set sweetener aside. Fill a large pitcher(s) with the seltzer. Using your wooden spoon, roughly stir in limes, next, mint leaves, then dissolved sweetener, and finally the rum. Stir, again, mixing all the ingredients. Fill your pitcher(s) half-way with crushed ice, and pour in your cocktail, stirring roughly once, again, to mix all the flavors together. Garnish each glass with a sprig of mint and serve immediately.

Strawberry-Raspberry Frozen Daquiris

Serves 4

> Not sure what to do with all of those summer berries that you have picked? Frozen, festive drinks for your get-together with friends are the perfect solution. Make one pitcher of daiquiris with alcohol and one without for the kids. At my house, the kids can pick the raspberries right from the bushes for these drinks (a really fun step for them). Use a blender specially made for frozen drinks to ensure the ice is crushed completely. Traditionally served in margarita glasses, any pretty wide-rimmed cocktail glass will do.
>
> *Story by Monica*

½ cup each fresh raspberries and strawberries
2 tablespoons lemon juice, freshly squeezed
½ cup powdered sugar or equivalent amount of stevia
2-4 tablespoons hot water
4 ounces flavored raspberry vodka
3 tablespoons lime juice, freshly squeezed
2 cups crushed ice
Extra berries for garnish

Make in 2 batches. Mix sugar or stevia with hot water until completely dissolved. Blend berries, dissolved sugar, and lemon juice into a puree. Strain out the seeds. Mix in 2 batches the crushed ice, vodka, puree, and lime juice, and blend until smooth. Pour into glasses and garnish with fresh berries, either sliced on the side of the glass or on a decorative plastic skewer along with a slice of lime for color. Serve immediately. Refrigerate between servings, and re-blend before re-freshing guests' cocktails.

Part IV

ENTRÉES AND SIDES

ENTRÉES AND SIDES

Come over for a barbeque. Let us load up the boat and sail to the beach for a clam bake and lobsters all around. There is a concert in the park tonight; let us pack the picnic basket and meet up at the entrance. Sound familiar? Light-hearted, spur of the moment dinner plans are a regular occurrence during the summer, accompanied by evenings spent lounging outdoors while talking, laughing, singing, and maybe even dancing under the moonlit sky.

Turn your evening backyard barbeque into a romantic scene straight out of an old movie with the soft glow of swaying paper lanterns, candlelight, and strings of fairy lights. As the grilled lamb slowly turns on a spit, set out your finest flowery china and colorful crystal, which says to your guests that this is a special night.

Serving a mix of several entrees is an annual tradition at Monica's house. Grilled Salmon (page 117) and marinated fillet mignon are delicious additions to her menu. Several sides, like a Greek Pasta Salad (page 51), Green Beans with Mustard and Shallot Vinaigrette (page 58), or Mary Elizabeth's Marinara Sauce (page 124) with pasta, offer your guests a varied and enticing choice of flavors: light, yet hearty; simple, yet elegant.

Cool down with pitchers of your signature cocktail, such as Minty Mojitos (page 94), accompanying grilled chicken fajitas with Guacamole (page 88). Frothy, Strawberry-Raspberry Frozen Daquiris (page 95), using berries hand-picked from your garden, can be served with or without alcohol to go with the kabobs.

On another balmy summer evening, turn your boating excursion into an overnight clambake on the beach. Clamming is still a popular pastime along many of our seashores. Step lightly and feel for the little mounds under the sand at sunrise, and dig up a delightful treat. For a traditional New England clambake, you will need lobsters with plenty of butter, boiled potatoes, and corn to go with your steamers. Singing around the bonfire on the beach and making s'mores are memories that your kids will keep for a lifetime. Camping along the National Seashore at Oregon Inlet in North Carolina, Monica remembers sharing their enormous catch of clams with other vacationers, who, in turn, would share their delicacies like smoked marlin, made with fish caught in the waters off the Outer Banks.

Exchanging old-time recipes like Southern Fried Chicken (page 104) or smoky barbeque ribs while sitting on the beach watching meteor showers in the August sky is sure to be a rewarding experience for all. Fill your picnic hamper to the delight of your family and friends on your next outing in the park with unique recipes that you have collected in your travels. Flavors using regional spices and herbs differ across the country, turning your meals into delectable journeys.

Treasure your lazy days of summer, whether at home or vacationing. Do your best to take the time to relax and treat yourself with fabulous food, surrounded by family, new and old friends, and, of course, fun in the sun.

Grandpa's Sauerkraut

Christian David Raiser *(Lynbrook, NY)*
Serves 8

1 medium green apple, chopped
1 small onion, chopped
1 small carrot, chopped
2 tablespoons butter
1 (16 oz.) bag sauerkraut, rinsed well
½ cup chicken broth
½ cup white wine (e.g., chardonnay)
½ teaspoon white vinegar

Sauté onion, apple, and carrot in butter for 10 minutes.

Add the remaining ingredients and simmer on low heat.

Add sugar to taste.

Leftovers may be stored in the refrigerator in a canning jar for 2 weeks.

Jamaican-Jerk Baked Beans

Gerarda Boger *(Southold, NY)*
Serves 8-10

> Here is a fun alternative to traditional baked beans, which Mary Elizabeth's sister makes for family barbeques.

1 ham steak, cut in ½-inch cubes
1 (15 oz.) can diced tomatoes, drained
1 (15 oz.) can pork and beans, rinsed and drained
1 (15 oz.) can black beans, rinsed and drained
1 (15 oz.) can white beans, rinsed and drained
1 large onion, chopped
1 large red bell pepper, chopped
1 large green pepper, chopped
½ cup packed dark brown sugar
½ cup cola
½ cup lemon-lime soda
1 teaspoon curry powder
½ teaspoon garlic powder
½ teaspoon cayenne powder
Sea salt and freshly cracked black pepper to taste

Place all the ingredients (except the salt and pepper) in a large, heavy pot. Bring to a boil over high heat. Reduce the heat to medium and simmer uncovered until the juices are thickened, stirring frequently and gently for about 45 minutes to an hour. Season with salt and pepper to taste.

Bread and Butter Slices

Susan Dodge *(Seaford, NY)*
Yields 8 pints

> A family tradition was started about thirty-five years ago, when my husband and I would attend the Long Island Old Bethpage Fair. This fair was held as far back as 1903, and consists of farm produce and animals grown and raised by Long Island farmers. People also entered homemade food, as well as arts and crafts.
>
> My husband enjoyed working in his backyard garden. He grew tomatoes, cucumbers, peppers, snap peas, pumpkins, and herbs. I used cucumbers from the garden and made bread and butter pickles to enter into the fair. To my delight and surprise, we won a first-place ribbon. That got us hooked, and I started a long line of entries. Many ribbons were won over the years by our children and our grandchildren, too.

4 quarts medium cucumbers, sliced
6 cups white onions, sliced
1⅔ cups green peppers, sliced
3 cloves garlic
⅓ cup pickling salt
Cracked ice

5 cups sugar
3 cups cider vinegar
2 tablespoons mustard seed
1½ teaspoons celery seed
1½ teaspoons ground turmeric

Combine cucumber, onion, green pepper, and whole garlic cloves. Add salt; cover with cracked ice. Mix thoroughly.

Let stand for 3 hours; drain well. Remove the garlic.

Combine the remaining ingredients and pour over the cucumber mixture. Bring to boiling. Fill hot pint jars with vegetables and liquid, leaving ½-inch of headspace. Adjust the lids.

Process in a boiling-water bath for 5 minutes (start counting time when the water returns to boiling).

Old-Fashioned Southern Fried Chicken

Serves 4

My first career was as a recreational therapist in nursing homes, where I met some of the most wonderful people who I have ever known. I used to write down their life stories for our resident newsletter, which also included a section of family recipes. I was informed that the only way to make true Southern fried chicken was to dip the chicken pieces in batter and fry it up. I have to agree, and have spent many a summer picnic enjoying it that way. I have changed the recipe over the years to suit my taste, like using extra virgin olive oil for frying. I began asking my butcher to cut up the chicken into 8-12 pieces the year that I made it for our family reunion on Labor Day weekend. The smaller pieces were easier to eat when balancing your plate and drink while sitting in a lawn chair.

Story by Monica

4-6 pounds chicken, cut into 8-12 pieces
2 cups flour
1-2 cups water
2 teaspoons sea salt, separated
1 teaspoon pepper, separated
1 teaspoon paprika (optional)
½-1 cup extra virgin olive oil

Wash and pat dry the cut-up chicken. Use 1 teaspoon of salt and ½ teaspoon of pepper to season the chicken. Make a watery paste with flour, water, the rest of the salt and pepper, and paprika (if using). Dip the chicken pieces in paste and place in a medium-high heated pan of olive oil. Brown for 3-4 minutes per side. Once all the pieces are browned, cook on medium to low, covered, until cooked through (about 20-30 minutes). Uncover and cook on high for the last 5-8 minutes, so the breading gets nice and crispy. Serve with a citrus fruit salad to counter the fat of the fried chicken.

Barbeque Sauce and Chicken

Chris and Lee Raiser *(Lynbrook, NY)*
Serves 4-6, Sauce Yields 2 cups

My parents made their own barbeque sauce, and I have never lost the taste for this tangy flavor. When I was growing up, one of my favorite summer dinners was when my dad cooked chicken on the backyard grill and lathered it with this sauce.

Story by Mary Elizabeth

Barbeque Sauce

2 medium onions, sliced
¼ cup extra virgin oil
2 (6 oz.) cans tomato paste
1 (28 oz.) can tomato puree
1 teaspoon sea salt
½ teaspoon pepper
1 teaspoon oregano
¼ cup worcestershire sauce

1 teaspoon dry mustard
2 teaspoons honey
½ cup red wine

Chicken

1 (3 pound) package of chicken thighs and legs

Barbeque Sauce

In a large frying pan, sauté the onions in olive oil until tender (about 10 minutes). Add all the ingredients, except the wine, and simmer for 5 minutes. Then add the wine and bring to a boil, boiling for 3 minutes.

Chicken

Wash and pat dry the chicken pieces; place on a grill with heat turned to medium. Once the barbeque sauce has cooled, brush it on the cooked chicken during the last 5 minutes of grilling.

Chef's Tip

If using frozen chicken defrost the chicken by putting it in the refrigerator the night before. It will be ready to prepare by dinnertime.

Grilled Chicken

Christine Melcher *(Hoagland, IN)*
Serves 6

> We grill out year around, but "no," we do not live where it is warm all year. Just pull the grill up to the back door; it is so worth the flavor even in the winter. I use the top-shelf of the grill, since I am usually cooking the rest of the meal in the house. If the grill flamed up and I did not see it, the chicken only gets a little flamed instead of charred. Being a busy mom, I always set the timer to avoid eating everything black. My husband likes to put some charcoal pieces in our propane gas grill; this gives the meat a wonderful flavor.

4-5 pieces of boneless, skinless chicken thighs
1 (12 oz.) can beer (any flavor)
½-1 cup Caribbean jerk-flavored marinade or any marinade
Seasoned salt to taste
Sea salt and freshly cracked black pepper to taste

Start the grill, setting the burners on high and heating it to around 350-400°F. Clean, separate, and trim the fat from the chicken. Place the chicken on the top shelf of the grill. Slowly pour a little bit of beer over each piece, letting it pool, if possible. Season with seasoned salt, salt, and pepper to taste. Close the lid and cook for 9 minutes. Turn the chicken pieces over. Repeat the beer, seasoned salt, salt, and pepper to taste. Close the lid, turn the burners down to medium, and cook for another 9 minutes. Turn the chicken, again, and put marinade on top. If you prefer plain chicken, just leave the marinade off. Close the lid and cook for 7 minutes. Turn the chicken and repeat the marinade step. Close the lid and cook for 7 minutes (if you have decided not to use the marinade, then the chicken may be done at this point). Check the chicken for doneness and remove from the grill.

Tandoori Chicken

Serves 4

> If you have read our books you know that I love Indian food,
> and try to turn many of my favorite dishes into an Indian one
> mainly using curry powder. Tandoori chicken is a flavorful
> grilled chicken that is delicious for a summer barbeque. Using
> aromatic spices, I have learned to prepare this dish. Now I can
> have it as often as I want.
>
> *Story by Monica*

3 pounds whole chicken,
cut into 8 pieces
Juice of 1 large lemon
2 tablespoons sea salt

Marinade
⅛ teaspoon ground cloves
2 teaspoons ground cumin
2 teaspoons coriander seeds,
crushed
10 cardamom seeds, crushed

2 onions, chopped
4 cloves garlic, finely chopped
3-inch piece of ginger, skinned
and finely chopped
1 teaspoon chili powder
½ teaspoon white pepper
1½ teaspoons turmeric
1 tablespoon paprika
½ teaspoon ground cinnamon
2 cups plain yogurt

Rinse the chicken and pat dry. Rub with lemon and salt inside and
out, and set aside. Roast the cloves, cumin, coriander, and cardamom for 10 minutes in a 400°F oven. Once cool, grind the coriander
and cardamom seeds with the ground cloves and cumin. Blend the
onions, garlic, and ginger, and then add chili powder, pepper, turmeric, paprika, cloves, and cinnamon; continue blending. Add the
yogurt and ground roasted spices, and strain in the lemon juice
from the chicken. Blend until smooth. Pour over the chicken in
a baking dish. Marinate in the refrigerator overnight, turning a
couple of times. Remove the chicken from the marinade, and boil
the marinade for 1-2 minutes. Place the chicken on a grill grate
for about 40-50 minutes, turning often. Brush the chicken with the
boiled marinade during the last 15 minutes of grilling. This dish
can be served hot or cold.

Spicy and Sweet Pan-Fried Chicken

Chef Shin Kim *(New York, NY)*
Serves 4-6

> The growing popularity of Korean chicken in recent years has inspired me to create an updated version. Here is one that combines what my mom used to whip up in a few minutes, which my sister and I devoured in an equal amount of time, with a friendlier version for home cooks.

Chicken

2 each legs, wings, and thighs
1 tablespoon ginger, freshly grated
Sea salt and freshly cracked black pepper to taste

Sauce

¼ cup gochu-jang (Korean red chili paste; see note below)
¼ cup ketchup
1 tablespoon sesame oil
1 tablespoon soy sauce
2 cloves garlic, grated
½ onion, grated
¼ cup corn syrup
2 tablespoons almonds, toasted and chopped (or any other nuts)
¼ cup each corn starch
¼ cup sweet rice flour (see note below) or all-purpose flour
Vegetable oil for frying

Chicken

Cut each thigh into 2-3 pieces. Wash all the chicken and pat dry with paper towels, then rubbing each piece with fresh grated ginger. Season with salt and pepper and let them rest for 30 minutes to an hour.

Sauce

Make the sauce by mixing gochu-jang, ketchup, sesame oil, soy sauce, garlic, and onion. Cook over low heat, stirring once in a while. You will see the sauce getting reduced and thicken slightly. Remove from the heat, add corn syrup, and stir to combine. Add toasted, chopped almonds and stir. Set aside.

Sift together corn starch and rice flour. Dredge the chicken pieces in this mixture, and place them on a hot pan with enough vegetable oil to cover the bottom of the pan. Fill up the pan with all the chicken pieces, if possible, to minimize oil-splattering. Pan-fry over medium-low heat to cook through without burning the skin of the meat. Flip once to the other side when the bottom part turns golden. Check for doneness when both sides are golden, which should be about 10 minutes of cooking.

Coat the chicken pieces in the sauce and mix well. Serve with rice.

Gochu-jang and sweet rice flour can be found in Asian grocery stores.

Chef's Tip

When frying, be sure to use an oil with a high smoke point (the point at which the oil gets so hot that it begins to smoke). Using an oil with a low smoke point will cause the product to burn, the flavor will deteriorate, and the food will taste bitter and burnt.

Ideal oils for deep-frying are grapeseed, canola, vegetable, peanut, safflower, and sunflower oils because they all have high smoke points. Examples of oils you should never use for frying would be olive or sesame oil. Try it next time and you will see a considerable difference!

For shallow frying, set the temperature at 300-325°F and make sure the oil is deep enough to cover the food at least halfway. This technique is ideal for food that needs to be cooked longer because it uses a smaller amount of oil at a lower temperature to ensure that the food will be fully cooked while obtaining the golden, crispy exterior. When you deep-fry, the product should be fully submerged in the oil to achieve that golden color and crisp texture. The appropriate temperature for deep-frying is 350-375°F. Once you see it start to smoke, it's too hot.

Fairway Market's Lamb Skewers with Yogurt Sauce

Danny Glickberg and Chef Mitchel London *(New York, NY)*
Serves 4

> Mitchel grew up in Israel, where lamb is everywhere. He used to visit a restaurant where he had some of the best food and was introduced to lamb skewers. Lamb is a great meat option for the grill in the summer, because it is full of flavor and is a nice change of pace from hamburgers and steaks. For a variation on this recipe, you can also add a pinch of coriander, ground fennel seeds, and chili pepper flakes into the marinade.

Lamb Skewers

2 tablespoons extra virgin olive oil
2 cloves garlic, smashed
1 sprig rosemary, stripped from sprig and chopped
Pinch each coriander, ground fennel seeds, and chili pepper flakes
1½ pounds leg of lamb, cut into 1-inch cubes
12 cherry tomatoes, red and yellow
8 shitake mushrooms, stems taken off
2 red onions, quartered
2 bunches scallions (use mostly white part)
1 red pepper, cut into squares
1 green pepper, cut into squares
Sea salt and freshly ground tellicherry or black pepper to taste

Yogurt Sauce

1 cup Greek yogurt
1 scallion, minced
1 clove garlic, crushed
2 tablespoons flat-leaf parsley, medium chopped
2 drops lemon juice, freshly squeezed
1 pinch sea salt

Lamb Skewers

Mix olive oil, garlic, rosemary, coriander, fennel seeds, chili pepper flakes, salt, and pepper in a large bowl. Add lamb, cover with plastic wrap, refrigerate, and allow to marinate overnight.

Arrange the skewers, alternating between lamb and vegetables. Heat a grill to a medium-high heat, place the skewers on the grill, and let sit for 1 minute. Turn the skewers over and let sit for another minute. Continue turning the skewers over every minute for 7-8 minutes total. If they are getting too charred, move them over to either side of the grill. Serve with yogurt sauce on the side.

Yogurt Sauce

Combine all the ingredients and refrigerate.

Chef's Tip

Know Your Ingredients

If you see green onions listed in your recipe, these are the same as scallions.

If you are unable to locate tellicherry peppercorns, you can substitute them with black peppercorns. Tellicherry peppercorns are actually black ones that have been left on the vine longer, developing a deeper, richer flavor. We always recommend, however, using a pepper mill and freshly grinding your pepper. The result will be a much more flavorful dish.

If the recipe calls for Greek yogurt, we do not recommend substituting it with regular yogurt. It will completely change the consistency of the finished product, since Greek yogurt is much thicker and smoother (similar to a custard).

Thai Grilled Leg of Lamb

Nancy Curry and Catherine Pepe, Temecula Olive Oil Company
(Temecula, CA)
Serves 2-4

> This savory lamb dish is full of flavor and is great when served fresh off the grill. For the ginger, we like to use a planer-style grater to get the most flavor. Fajita Frenzy is a fabulous Persian-lime olive oil and, like all our oils, the fresh lime is crushed with the olives.

1 large chunk ginger, peeled and grated
4 cloves garlic
1 bunch fresh cilantro leaf tops (no stems), some reserved for garnish
1-2 jalapeño peppers, roughly chopped and seeded
4 tablespoons Temecula Olive Oil Company Fajita Frenzy Olive Oil
1-2 pound leg of lamb, butterflied (you can ask your butcher to do this)
Juice of 1 lime

Preheat your oven to 325°F. Grind the ginger, garlic, cilantro, and peppers in a food processor to a thick paste. Add oil at the end and pulse just to combine. Place lamb in a roasting pan and rub on the marinade. If you have time, refrigerate for an hour, but if not, you will still get a lot of flavor. Cover with tin foil and bake for 1 hour. About a half-hour into your cooking time, light your charcoal grill and let it die down a bit. Grill the lamb for about 10 minutes, until you get the level of char and crust that you like. Carve the lamb into chunky slices and top with cilantro and lime juice.

Grilled Teriyaki Lamb Chops

Amy Ott *(Greenfield, IN)*
Serves 4-6

¼ cup teriyaki sauce
2 tablespoons water
1 tablespoon vegetable oil
1 tablespoon brown sugar
½ teaspoon each freshly cracked black pepper and garlic powder
8 lamb chops

Mix all the ingredients together to make a marinade. Place the lamb chops in 9- by 12-inch dish. Pour the marinade over the lamb chops, cover with plastic wrap, refrigerate, and let sit for 10-12 hours. Pour off the marinade and grill to desired doneness.

Fairway Market's Cornish Game Hen

Danny Glickberg and Chef Mitchel London *(New York, NY)*
Serves 1

> Roasted chicken is about as simple as cooking gets. There is nothing better than a roasted chicken when you prepare it and eat it immediately. It is economical and delicious. There is a farmer's market in the south of France that is full of roasted chicken, and this recipe is an adaptation of some roasted chickens from that market. Try adding some potatoes to the pan, and we guarantee that they will be delicious.

1 Cornish game hen
¼ cup extra virgin olive oil
1 clove garlic, crushed
2 Thai chili peppers, crushed
Juice of 2 lemons
Zest of 1 lemon
3 sprigs fresh oregano, chopped
3 springs fresh cilantro for garnish
Sea salt and freshly cracked tellicherry or black pepper to taste

Mix all the ingredients (except cilantro) to make a marinade. Marinate the hen in a bowl for 24-48 hours. Over medium heat, place the hen skin-side-down in the middle of the grill for 10-15 minutes. Flip the hen over, placing it on the side of the grill, and grilling for 10-15 minutes more. Serve by adding more lemon juice, a drizzle of olive oil, and garnish with the cilantro.

Fairway Market's Grilled Red Snapper

Danny Glickberg and Chef Mitchel London *(New York, NY)*
Serves 1

Juice of 1 lime
Zest of 1 lime
¼ cup extra virgin olive oil
½ handful cilantro leaves for marinade
4-5 Thai chili peppers, crushed with the back of your knife
Pinch sea salt
¼ pound red snapper, cut into strips
2-3 cilantro leaves for garnish
1 bunch baby arugula or Bibb lettuce

In a shallow bowl, combine all the ingredients (except arugula, lettuce, and cilantro) to create a marinade. Coat red snapper strips well and allow to marinate for 3-4 hours.

Get your grill hot. Grill the fish meat-side-down for 2-3 minutes. Flip and grill on the skin-side for 2-3 minutes. Serve over a bed of baby arugula or Bibb lettuce. Drizzle with olive oil and garnish with 2-3 cilantro leaves.

Grilled Swordfish with Spiced Red Pepper Sauce

Chef Sonali Ruder *(New York, NY)*

Serves 4

1½ teaspoons cumin seeds
1½ teaspoons coriander seeds
1 (7 oz.) jar roasted red peppers, drained
1 clove garlic
1 tablespoon lemon juice, freshly squeezed
¼ teaspoon red pepper flakes
2 tablespoons vegetable oil, plus extra to brush on fish
4 (6 oz.) swordfish steaks
2 tablespoons cilantro, chopped
Lemon wedges for garnish
Sea salt and freshly cracked black pepper to taste

Preheat a gas or charcoal grill to medium-high heat.

Lightly toast the cumin and coriander seeds in a small skillet on the stove over medium-low heat until fragrant. Place the spices in a blender along with the red peppers, garlic, lemon juice, red pepper flakes, and vegetable oil. Blend until smooth and set aside. Season with salt and pepper to taste.

Brush the swordfish steaks with oil and season them with salt and pepper to taste. Grill the steaks for 3-4 minutes on each side until cooked through. Transfer them to a serving platter and top them with the spiced red pepper sauce. Garnish with cilantro and lemon wedges.

Grilled Salmon

Serves 4

> Salmon can be grilled plain with a little lemon or lime juice,
> a teaspoon of mayonnaise and chopped dill, and tastes
> phenomenal. I serve it fairly often, and try all different kinds of
> ways to prepare it. Grilled on the barbeque on a plank of cedar
> has to be one of the tastiest ways to have salmon, and you may
> never go back to any other way of cooking it.
>
> *Story by Monica*

Glaze
⅛ cup maple syrup
1 tablespoon orange juice
1 rice wine
1 tablespoon hoisin sauce
3 tablespoons teriyaki sauce
2 inches fresh ginger, grated
1 clove garlic, grated
1 tablespoon garlic powder
1 tablespoon onion powder

Salmon
Cooking-grade cedar plank with warm water to cover
2 pounds salmon fillets
1 tablespoon extra virgin olive oil

Glaze
Mix all ingredients for the glaze in a bowl and set aside.

Salmon

Soak your cooking-grade cedar planks in warm water for approximately 2 hours before using. Place the salmon filet skin side down on plank on grilling grate over an indirect flame. Close the lid and grill for about 20-30 minutes over medium heat. Add a glaze about 7-10 minutes before taking off the grill. Refrigerate any leftover glaze, which can be used again on chicken, beef, or pork.

You can make a glaze from your favorite herbs and spices combined with liquid like juice or teriyaki sauce, and use on a variety of meats and even vegetables. Depending on the herbs that you use, you can have an Asian flavor as in the recipe above; Italian, using garlic, onion, oregano, basil, olive oil, and honey; or Mexican, using chili sauce, cayenne pepper flakes, garlic, onion, cilantro, cumin, and chili powder. Making a marinade is similar, though you will want more liquid and lemon juice or vinegar to tenderize. Soak your meat for varied amounts of time: anywhere from 20 minutes for chicken tenders to overnight for a London broil. Do not use the marinade to baste, unless you have boiled it for a couple of minutes once removing the meat from it. Using a rub is another way of flavoring and tenderizing your meat, like ribs or steaks. You can create your own rubs using different spice combinations. Rubs are used to rub into meats and are primarily used for slow-cooking or smoking. You do not have to own a smoker to enjoy the tenderness or flavor of one. You can use a couple of teaspoons of hickory flavor to your rub or marinade and get the same effect. Slow-cooking a rack of ribs on 200°F in your oven for 10-12 hours, depending on their size, and then grilling will result in nice, tender ribs. You can marinate them with the boiled down juice from the slow-cooking once on the grill. Adding a little beer to the slow-cooking process will further tenderize the meat.

Pinchito de Mar (Grilled Seafood Skewer)

Chef Sebastian Cambeiro *(New York, NY)*
Makes 3- 4 skewers

Marinade
1 teaspoon Spanish paprika
1½ ounces lemon juice, freshly squeezed
3 garlic cloves, smashed
Sea salt and freshly ground black and white pepper to taste

Seafood (3 per skewer)
1 octopus
10 clams
10 oysters
¼-½ pound baby calamari (tentacles can be used for this recipe)

Precook the octopus until it is fork-tender or easily pierced by a toothpick. Let the octopus cool for an hour, or, it can be saved a night ahead.

In a bowl, marinate all the seafood with paprika, lemon juice, garlic cloves, salt, and peppers. Keep the marinated seafood in the refrigerator for at least 1 hour. Then carefully place one-by-one on to each skewer, alternating.

Meanwhile, as you are preparing the skewers, heat the grill to medium-high temperature (make sure that it is not too hot, because seafood can easily overcook). This can also be barbequed.

Place each skewer individually onto the grill, leaving some room between each skewer. Cook for about 6-8 minutes (checking by simply touching to see if the seafood is properly cooked).

Summer Garden Zucchini Carpaccio

Lisa Rosenberg *(Park Slope, Brooklyn, NY)*
Serves 4

> Uncooked dinners, preferably those featuring produce bought from the farmers market or picked from the garden, are my favorite kind of summer dinner. Fresh, crusty bread with salad and local seasonal fruit are the perfect accompaniments, as is a Long Island wine.

4 small zucchinis or 2-3 larger ones (1 pound total)
⅓ cup loosely packed, fresh mixed-herb leaves (no stems)
2 tablespoons extra-virgin olive oil
2 teaspoons fresh lemon juice
¼ teaspoon fine sea salt
¼ cup pine nuts (approximately 1 ounce), toasted
4-6 ounces parmigiano-reggiano (can substitute grana padano or another very hard cheese)
Freshly cracked pepper to taste

Cut zucchini diagonally into paper-thin slices with a mandolin or very sharp large-blade knife. If you are in a hurry, you can use the largest, thinnest slicing blade of a food processor (the thinness is crucial, and the slices should be almost translucent). Arrange the slices, overlapping slightly, in a single layer on small serving plates or 1 large serving plate.

Stack herbs and cut crosswise into very thin slivers, and then sprinkle over the zucchini.

Whisk together oil and lemon juice in a small bowl, and drizzle over the zucchini. Sprinkle lightly with salt, remembering the saltiness of the cheese. Grind on a few turns of fresh pepper.

Sprinkle with pine nuts. Let stand for 10 minutes to soften the zucchini and allow the flavors to develop. Just before serving, use a vegetable peeler to shave the cheese into narrow strips to taste over the zucchini.

Thai Peanut Noodles

Nancy Curry and Catherine Pepe, Temecula Olive Oil Company
(Temecula, CA)
Serves 6

1 pound cooked udon noodles
4 tablespoons Temecula Olive Oil Company Picante Pepper Olive
Oil (separated)
4 cloves garlic, sliced
1-inch ginger, peeled and roughly chopped
¼ cup soy sauce
½ cup peanut butter
¼ cup Temecula Olive Oil Company Balsamico Bianco (or rice vinegar)
3 green onions, finely chopped
½ cup peanuts, chopped

Cook the noodles according to the package directions. When ready
to drain, reserve a little of the pasta water. In a large bowl, toss the
cooled pasta with 2 tablespoons of oil to coat evenly. In a food processor, pulse garlic and ginger until minced. Add the remaining
ingredients (except oil, green onions, and peanuts), and pulse until
smooth. Add the rest of the oil, and pulse just to combine. Toss well
with the noodles, adding the pasta water if necessary. Top with
green onions and peanuts.

Pesto Bowtie Pasta

Yields 2 cups of pesto; serves 6

My dear friend Lorraine generously dove into her recipe collection to share recipes with us for the *Country Comfort* series. She is an avid gardener and loves to cook. This recipe combines both of her passions. After picking the basil at the end of summer, Lorraine makes pesto for her family to enjoy through the coming months.

Story by Mary Elizabeth

2 cups tightly packed fresh basil leaves
½ cup extra virgin olive oil
½ cup grated Parmesan cheese
2 tablespoons pine nuts
1 tablespoon fresh garlic, minced
1 teaspoon sea salt
1 pound bowtie pasta

Process all the ingredients (except pasta) in a food processor for 2-3 minutes. Make pasta according to the package directions. Toss with enough pesto to coat. The recipe freezes well. Place 1 cup in a plastic container and cover with a layer of olive oil before freezing.

Linguine with Asparagus and Pine Nuts

Bizzy and Kathy Acierno *(Sayville, NY)*
Serves 4-6

My friend Kathy's daughter Bizzy, aged 12, wants to become a chef. Her favorite show is Cake Boss. She comes from a family of great cooks. Her grandmother, Dorothy Acierno, and aunt, Miss Amy, both have recipes in our books. So, we were very happy when she wanted to publish a recipe of her own, which she had adapted from a magazine for our *Summer Favorites* book.

Story by Monica

1 pound linguine
¼ cup extra virgin olive oil
¼ cup pine nuts
4 cloves garlic, sliced
2 pounds fresh asparagus, trimmed and cut into 1-inch pieces
Kosher salt and freshly cracked black pepper to taste
1 cup rotisserie chicken, shredded
1 cup shaved Parmesan cheese

Cook the pasta according to the package directions. Heat the oil, adding the pine nuts and garlic, stirring frequently until golden (about 2 minutes). Add in the asparagus and cook for about 3 minutes. Add the mixture to the pasta along with salt and pepper. Toss with chicken and then sprinkle cheese before serving.

Marinara Sauce

Serves 6

When you walk in the front door of my sister-in-law Patti's home, you are always greeted by the aroma of a fresh sauce simmering on the stove. You know that it has been lovingly made with fresh tomatoes from their farm. After starting a landscaping business, her husband and town mayor, Butch Starkie, went on to purchase a 100-year-old farmhouse, surrounded by acres of land to grow his own trees and shrubs, and opened up a garden center. Consequently, his fresh tomatoes taste as sweet as candy. Once you eat them picked off the vine, it is hard to go back to the store-bought version. We all love to reap the benefits of his fresh produce, especially their homemade tomato sauce, which they make every August and use throughout the entire year.

Story by Mary Elizabeth

3 tablespoons extra virgin olive oil
2 small onions, chopped
1 garlic clove, minced
2½ cups roma tomatoes, peeled, seeded, and diced
½ tablespoon fresh oregano, finely chopped, or ½ teaspoon dried oregano, crumbled
¼ teaspoon sugar
1 fresh basil leaf or a pinch of dried basil, crumbled
Sea salt and freshly cracked black pepper to taste

Heat oil in heavy, medium saucepan over medium heat. Add onions and garlic, and sauté until translucent (about 10 minutes). Add tomatoes, oregano, sugar, and basil. Simmer until thickened for about 1 hour, stirring occasionally. Season with salt and pepper to taste.

Sicilian Summer Pasta Sauce

Christian David Raiser *(Lynbrook, NY)*
Serves 6-8

I am sharing one of my dad's recipes below, which was first featured in the "Food Day" section of our Long Island newspaper, Newsday. It was originally made by my mom's mother, Grandma Navoni. As often happens, however, she never wrote it down. My dad painstakingly worked at trying to replicate it. Growing up, it was one of our favorites, especially since he used fresh mint from our garden, and served it at room temperature, making it the perfect dinner on a hot summer's night. In our house, it is especially meaningful, having spanned over the generations, from my grandmother down to my daughter Nicole, who recently added clams, and features it on the menus in the restaurants that she has worked in. This one is very easy and requires no cooking at all.

Story by Mary Elizabeth

1 (28 oz.) can plum tomatoes, coarsely chopped
¼ cup extra virgin olive oil
3 cloves garlic, chopped
½ cup loosely packed fresh mint leaves, chopped
½ teaspoon sea salt
½ teaspoon freshly cracked black pepper
¼ cup dry white wine
1 pound cooked pasta

Mix all the ingredients, except the pasta, in a bowl. Set aside in a refrigerator (it is best after 1-2 days). Just before serving, bring the sauce to room temperature. Pour over the cooked pasta.

New York Strip Steaks with Avocado Butter and Charred Corn Salsa

Chef Sonali Ruder *(New York, NY)*
Serves 6

Charred Corn Salsa

4 ears corn, silks and husks removed
2 tablespoons plus 1 teaspoon canola oil, separated
¼ cup red onion, finely chopped
3 tablespoons cilantro, chopped
2 tablespoons lime juice, freshly squeezed
½ teaspoon ground cumin
Kosher salt and freshly cracked black pepper to taste

Steak

6 boneless, beef top-loin (strip) steaks, about 1-inch thick
Canola oil

Avocado Butter

1 large, ripe Haas avocado, peeled and pitted
4 tablespoons unsalted butter, softened
1 clove garlic, chopped
1 tablespoon cilantro, chopped
1 tablespoon lime juice, freshly squeezed
Kosher salt and freshly cracked black pepper to taste

Preheat a gas grill over medium-high heat and brush the grill rack with approximately 1 tablespoon of oil.

Charred Corn Salsa

To make the charred corn salsa, drizzle each piece of corn with 1 teaspoon of canola oil and place them on the grill. Cook, turning occasionally, until the corn is lightly charred on all sides.

Cut the kernels off the cobs and mix them in a bowl with the onion, 3 tablespoons of cilantro, 2 tablespoons of lime juice, cumin, and 1 tablespoon of canola oil. Season with salt and pepper to taste. Set aside.

Steak

Pat the steaks dry and drizzle them with canola oil. Season each steak on both sides with salt and pepper. Place the steaks on the grill, and cook for 10-12 minutes for medium-rare to medium doneness, turning occasionally. Remove the steaks and let them rest.

Avocado Butter

While the steaks are grilling, make the avocado butter by pureeing the avocado, butter, garlic, cilantro, and lime juice until smooth. Season with salt and pepper to taste.

Serve steaks on a bed of charred corn salsa topped with dollops of avocado butter.

Grilled Flat Iron Steaks with Sun-Dried Tomato Chimichurri

Chef Sonali Ruder *(New York, NY)*
Serves 4

¼ cup extra virgin olive oil
¼ cup sun-dried tomatoes, packed in oil, finely chopped
2 tablespoons oil from the jar of sun-dried tomatoes
4 cloves garlic, sliced very thin
3 tablespoons balsamic vinegar
¼ cup fresh parsley, chopped
4 (8 oz.) shoulder top-blade (flat iron) steaks, cut 1-inch thick
Kosher salt and freshly cracked black pepper to taste

Preheat a gas or charcoal grill over medium-high heat.

Heat the olive oil, sun-dried tomatoes, 2 tablespoons of sun-dried tomato oil, and garlic in a medium frying pan over medium heat for 3-4 minutes, until the flavors are infused into the oil. Pour the mixture into a medium bowl and stir in the balsamic vinegar, parsley, salt, and pepper to taste. Set aside.

Season the steaks generously with salt and pepper on both sides. Grill the steaks, covered, for 11-14 minutes for medium-rare to medium doneness, turning occasionally. Let the meat rest, and then slice across the grain. Arrange slices on a platter topped with the sun-dried tomato chimichurri.

Traditional Macaroni and Cheese

Chef Benny Franklin *(Southampton, NY)*
Serves 10-15

This recipe originated in Virginia and was brought to New York by my grandmother, Helen L. Johnson, who later passed it down to her daughter, Hazel S. Johnson, and then passed down to my siblings and I. Back in the 1950s, this macaroni and cheese was prepared on a large, black wooden stove on a farm in my hometown. It consisted of milk straight from the cow, homemade butter, eggs from the chickens, and cheeses from the local markets. Since the original recipe, we have enhanced the flavor with other seasonings. We still prepare it on Sundays and holidays for our family and friends when they come to visit us from different parts of the country.

2 sticks salted butter
4 (6 oz.) cans evaporated milk
4 (10 oz.) blocks extra-sharp cheddar cheese (or any cheese), shredded and separated
2 egg yolks
1½ pounds elbow macaroni
6 ounces water or ½ pint half-and-half
Sea salt and freshly cracked white pepper to taste
Garlic powder to taste (optional)
Paprika to taste (optional)

Preheat an oven to 375°F.

Melt butter in a pot on low heat; after the butter is melted, add evaporated milk and stir. Once mixed, add 3 of the 4 blocks of cheese to the mix, stirring on low heat until melted. Add the cheese in a little at a time until melted.

Once melted, take the sauce off the heat and add the 2 yolks one at a time, whisking fast until blended. Add salt and white pepper to taste, and garlic powder, if using.

You want the sauce to nappe (a la nappe is an ideal consistency for most sauces; you know that it is done if you are able to drag a line across the back of a spoon).

For a thicker consistency, add a roux a little at a time to thicken the sauce (see Chef's Tip on page 167).

Once the sauce is complete to your liking, layer the mix with the macaroni by adding the sauce, next, the macaroni, and then the remaining shredded cheese.

To give the macaroni some color, sprinkle paprika on top of the macaroni and cheese before baking. Bake for 45 minutes to 1 hour.

Smoked Gouda Macaroni and Cheese

A Silverware Affair *(Chattanooga, TN)*
Serves 12

> Here is an alternative to the classic dish. As suggested by Tara from A Silverware Affair, you can alter it even further by substituting equal amounts American cheese for the cheddar and bleu cheese for the gouda. The sauce is also versatile, and is great over chicken or mashed potatoes, mixed in salsa for a dip, or poured over steamed broccoli. It has endless possibilities.

2 tablespoons flour
½ cup butter, softened
1 cup heavy cream
8 ounces cheddar cheese, shredded
8 ounces gouda cheese, shredded
½ teaspoon garlic, minced
1 teaspoon each sea salt and freshly cracked black pepper
4 cups cooked pasta (bowtie or penne)

Mix flour and butter over medium heat to form a roux. Once formed, add heavy cream and stir, heating thoroughly.

Then add cheddar and gouda cheese and stir until melted. Add garlic, salt, and pepper, altering to taste.

Pour sauce over 4 cups of pasta.

The Pig Roast

Elizabeth Sullivan *(Sayville, NY)*
Serves 8

It all started as a casual backyard barbeque at our house one lazy end-of-summer day in September. My friends and I decided that we would collect donations and give them to a good cause. We collected a couple thousand dollars and donated it to several charities in our area.

It has since become a tradition that gets bigger every year. My friend at the local newspaper wrote a story about it; word got out about our charity, and we eventually had to move out of our yard and onto the grounds of a local organization. Today, local restaurant owners pitch in as well by donating all the food and drink. No one gets paid a penny: all proceeds go to the charities. This year, 800 people came, and we collected $70,000.

One of our attendees asked if we could handle 2,000 people, so, we are now readying ourselves for a much larger event next year. One of the greatest parts of it is we all have fun while we are working together for a good cause. See Chef's Tips (page 161) for tips on how to roast a pig.

Part V

DESSERTS

DESSERTS

Besides the traditional barbeques and picnics, summer also brings to mind "June brides." Living on Long Island, summertime is ideal for hosting weddings overlooking the Great South Bay, or, for sitting poolside at a backyard bridal shower. A signature gift seems fitting for making a lasting imprint of these special events. After attending culinary school for baking and the pastry arts, Mary Elizabeth started to give each new bride a gift that would remind them of her: a clear, glass cake stand with a dome cover. She always accompanies it with a few of her favorite classic dessert recipes, like her Chocolate Chip Cookies (page 144). It is easy and fun to make recipe cards by purchasing colored sheets of card stock to coordinate with the wrapping paper. Trim it to 3- by 5-inches using craft scissors, creating a whimsical edge; punch a hole in the upper left hand corner; string contrasting ribbon through; and attach each to the bow.

When displaying desserts for backyard picnics, Mary Elizabeth and Monica equally enjoy the preparation and presentation of the finished products. Part of the fun is in lining up cookies handsomely on a decorative dish, and telling the hostess that the dish is hers to keep long after the crumbs are all gone. It is a special, yet simple way to thank a friend or family member for bringing you into their home.

One of our favorite holidays to do this for is the Fourth of July. There is always a big selection of patriotic cloth napkins to drape over colored baskets, filled with Carol's One-Bowl Brownies (page 145), wrapped in clear cellophane and tied with a royal-blue ribbon adorned with stars. Summer is the perfect time to bring a dessert to a picnic and savor cool, light sweets and luscious fresh fruits from the recipes that you will find on the following pages.

Cheesecake

Karen Fricke *(Blue Point, NY)*
Serves 10

> Whenever we go to our friend Karen's house for a party, we know dessert will always include her famous cheesecake. It is one of the creamiest that I have ever had.
>
> *Story by Mary Elizabeth*

1 (8 oz.) tub whipped cream cheese
1 stick unsalted butter
16 ounces sour cream
5 eggs
1 teaspoon vanilla extract
2 tablespoons corn starch
1 teaspoon lemon juice
1½ cups sugar

Allow the cream cheese, butter, sour cream, and eggs to come to room temperature. In a large mixing bowl, blend together all the ingredients, except the eggs. Beat the eggs into the mixture one at a time, mixing well after each addition. Pour mixture into a greased 10-inch spring-form pan. Place the pan in a large roasting pan that has been half-filled with hot water. Cover the bottom of spring-form pan with aluminum foil to catch any leaks. Bake at 375°F in the oven for 1 hour. Remove from the oven to cool.

Strawberry and Rhubarb Sauce

Makes 3 cups

When I taste this sauce, it brings me right back to my childhood. Each summer, my dad would pick fresh rhubarb from our neighbor's garden. At the time, he used a pressure cooker to make his sauce, which we enjoyed over vanilla ice cream or cheesecake. I always looked forward to it, since I savored the tart and sweet flavor combination.

Story by Mary Elizabeth

¼-½ cup sugar, depending on desired tartness
¼ cup water
1 pound rhubarb stalks, diced
1 quart strawberries, hulled and quartered
1 teaspoon vanilla extract
4 drops red food coloring (optional)

In a large saucepan over medium heat, combine the sugar and water. Stir just until the sugar is dissolved. Add rhubarb, strawberries, and vanilla extract, and then stir. Cover and cook on low for 30 minutes. If using food coloring, stir it in just before serving.

Raspberry and Peach Pie

Lorraine Ott *(Boxford, MA)*
Serves 6

1 pre-baked pie shell
4 pounds fresh peaches
1 cup raspberry jam, seedless (preferably homemade or the best quality you can get)
¼ teaspoon cinnamon
1 teaspoon sugar
¼ pound butter, cut into 1-tablespoon pieces

Boil water and add peaches for 2-3 minutes. Drain, cool, and remove the skins, cutting each into 6-8 pieces, and putting into a large bowl. Mix in raspberry jam, cinnamon, and sugar, and toss until blended. Pour the filling into the pie shell and dot butter on the filling before baking. Bake at 350°F for 20 minutes or until bubbly.

Strawberries Napoleon

Christine Melcher (Hoagland, IN)

> I happened upon this recipe in search for a good strawberry trifle recipe using puffed pastry. All the recipes that I found used sponge cake, angel-food cake, or jelly rolls. Instead, I purchased a box of frozen puffed pastry sheets, and used a trifle bowl to present the dessert.

1 (17.3 oz.) package frozen puffed pastry sheets
1 (3.9 oz.) package French vanilla instant-pudding mix
1 cup whole milk
1 teaspoon raspberry-flavored liquor (optional)
1 (8 oz.) tub whipped cream
1 cup powdered sugar
4 teaspoons whole milk
4 cups fresh strawberries, sliced or raspberries

Thaw 2 pastry sheets to room temperature (about 40 minutes). Heat an oven to 400°F, and line a baking sheet with parchment paper. Unfold the pastries, using 1⅓ of the sheets (you can refreeze the remaining pastry), and then cut the 1-piece into 9 squares and the ⅓-piece into 3 pieces.

Place on baking sheets and bake for 15 minutes (pastries will be a light-golden color)

Cool on a wire rack. Whisk milk into the pudding mix and raspberry liquor for at least 1 minute. Fold whipped cream into the pudding mix, cover, and refrigerate. Stir powdered sugar and 4 teaspoons of milk to make an icing. Split each pastry into 2 layers, forming 24 squares. Place 8 puffed pieces in the bottom of a trifle bowl. Drizzle about ¼ of icing over the puffs. Layer ⅓ of the pudding mixture. Layer ⅓ of the strawberry slices. Repeat these layers 2 more times

Drizzle the remaining icing over top of the dish.

Lemon Cookies

Nancy Curry and Catherine Pepe, Temecula Olive Oil Company
(Temecula, CA)
Makes 4 dozen cookies

> This is a family favorite. These can be served with fresh berries macerated and drizzled with Temecula Olive Oil Company Vanilla Fig Balsamic Vinegar.

2 cups flour
1 cup plus 2 tablespoons sugar
½ teaspoon baking soda
½ cup plus 2 tablespoons Temecula Olive Oil Company D'Luscious Lemon Olive Oil
2 tablespoons milk
1 tablespoon lemon zest
Juice from 1 large lemon

Preheat the oven to 350°F. Line 2 baking sheets with parchment paper. Sift together the first 3 ingredients into a medium bowl. Stir the remaining ingredients together in a separate small bowl. Add together all the ingredients, stirring until the mixture comes together. Place 2 tablespoons of sugar in a small bowl. To make the cookies, pinch off a teaspoon of dough and roll into balls approximately 1 inch in diameter. Roll the balls in sugar and place them 2 inches apart on the baking sheets. Bake the cookies, one sheet at a time, until cooked through and very lightly browned (about 12-15 minutes). Be careful not to over-bake: the cookies will be soft to the touch and have a crackled surface when done. With a wide metal spatula, transfer the cookies to a wire rack to cool completely. Store in an air-tight container.

Ice Cream Cake

Gretel Carlin, *(Stony Brook, NY)*
Serves 12-16

> My sister-in-law delighted us all one year, when she made a homemade ice cream cake for her son's June birthday. He was so surprised, and we were all impressed by her daring feat. It was eaten up in an instant, and has been a birthday favorite at her house ever since.
>
> *Story by Monica*

9- by 13-inch baking dish
2 quarts your favorite ice cream
1 row Oreo® cookies (about 15-20), crushed
1 (18 oz.) jar hot fudge
1 (14 oz.) can whipped cream

Spread crushed Oreos on the bottom of a baking dish. Spread 1 quart of softened ice cream, the hot fudge, and then the other quart of ice cream. Place in the freezer for several hours. Just before serving, spray whipped cream on top and enjoy. Variations: add different kinds of ice cream for each layer, a layer of cherries or strawberries, or a different kind of cookie, like vanilla wafers or ginger cookies.

Stone Fruit Torte

Chef Nicole Roarke *(Blue Point, NY)*
Serves 6

> Like most chefs, Nicole prefers cooking to baking, especially since cooking does not rely as heavily on a recipe and precise measurements. When it comes to dessert, she was quick to offer her clients a fresh fruit and cheese platter. Now that she works as an executive chef and a chef instructor at a culinary school, she has had to come out of her comfort zone and start preparing desserts. We are glad that she has. Here is one of her recipes that our family loves.
>
> *Story by Mary Elizabeth*

6 Italian plums, halved, pitted, and thinly sliced
6 nectarines, halved, pitted, and thinly sliced
1 teaspoon lemon juice, freshly squeezed
1 teaspoon cinnamon
1 teaspoon sugar
½ cup unsalted butter, softened
2 eggs
1 pinch sea salt
1 cup sugar
1 cup flour
1 teaspoon baking powder
Whipped cream for garnish
1 tablespoon confectioner's sugar for garnish

Preheat an oven to 350°F. Place fruit in a mixing bowl, and toss with lemon juice, cinnamon, and 1 teaspoon of sugar. Set aside. Cream butter and 1 cup of sugar together. Add the remaining ingredients, beating well.

Spoon into a 9-inch, greased spring-form pan. Bake at 350°F for 1 hour. Once cool, remove the pan, and slice into 8 portions. Garnish with fresh whipped cream and confectioner's sugar.

Angel-Food Cake with Chocolate Shavings

Lorraine Ott *(Boxford, MA)*
Serves 8

1¼ cups cake flour
1½ cups superfine sugar, separated
14 large egg whites, room temperature
1¼ teaspoons cream of tartar
1 cup chocolate shavings (use a mixture of milk, bittersweet, and semisweet chocolate shavings; see note below)

Heat an oven to 350°F. Prepare a bundt pan by generously spraying with baking spray (see Baker's Tips on page 170). Sift flour into a bowl, and then resift with ¾ cup of sugar.

Beat whites until frothy, add cream of tartar, and mix until it comes to 3 times the original size (about 3 minutes). Slowly add ¾ cup of sugar, and beat for 2 minutes more on high until firm and glossy.

Gently fold in the flour mixture in 3 additions. Then fold in chocolate shavings. Pour into the bundt pan. Bake for 40-45 minutes or until the top is golden-brown.

As an alternative, substitute ½ cup of white chocolate shavings and ½ cup of fresh raspberries or 1 cup of raspberries alone.

Chocolate Chip Cookies

Makes 2 dozen cookies

When it comes to desserts, I am always on the quest to find what I think is the best recipe for the traditional classics. I have tried multiple chocolate chip cookie recipes over the years, but this one has now become my favorite. Picnics are a perfect time to serve them, since they are easy to pack and are enjoyed by all ages.

Story by Mary Elizabeth

1 cup butter, softened
1 cup sugar
½ cup brown sugar
3 eggs
2 teaspoons vanilla extract
2 cups flour
1 teaspoon baking soda
1½ teaspoons sea salt
2 cups semisweet chocolate chips
1 cup broken walnuts (optional)

Preheat an oven to 350°F. Beat the first 5 ingredients until light and fluffy (approximately 3 minutes on high). Sift together flour, baking soda, and salt. Blend the flour mixture into the sugar mixture. Gently stir in chips and chopped nuts (if using) with a wooden spoon. Drop cookies by the scoopful approximately 3 inches apart on a cookie sheet covered with parchment paper. Bake for about 8-10 minutes. When slightly cooled, use a spatula, take the cookies off the cookie sheet, and cool on wire racks.

If you prefer a crisper cookie, refrigerate the dough for 1 hour before baking, and always try to use a good-quality pure vanilla extract and chocolate.

Brownies

Makes 2 dozen 2-inch squares4

My friend Carol conducts cooking classes in her backyard cooking studio. She creates a beautiful scene with her picture-perfect yard filled with benches, raspberry vines, and a fresh vegetable and herb garden. For one of her demonstrations, she made these brownies, which are rich, chewy, and easy to make. I have added coffee crystals to enhance the chocolate flavor. Above all, this is now my favorite "go-to" brownie recipe.

Story by Mary Elizabeth

2 sticks unsalted butter
8 ounces bittersweet chocolate (use a good-quality chocolate such as Ghirardelli or Valrhona)
4 large eggs
½ teaspoon sea salt
1 cup sugar
1 cup packed brown sugar
2 teaspoons vanilla extract
1 teaspoon instant coffee crystals (optional)
1 cup flour
1½ cups pecans, coarsely chopped (optional)

Preheat an oven to 350°F with the rack in the center. Spray the bottom and sides of a 9- by 13-inch pan generously with baking spray, line with parchment, and spray, again. Melt chocolate and butter in a double boiler or heat-proof bowl set over a pot, in which the water has boiled, and the heat is off. Remove from the heat and stir until the chocolate is thoroughly combined with the butter.

In a large bowl, whisk eggs, and then whisk in salt, sugars, vanilla, and coffee. Using a wooden spoon, stir in the chocolate and butter mixture, and then fold in the flour and nuts. Pour the batter into a prepared pan, spreading evenly. Bake for about 45 minutes. Cool on a wire rack. When completely cooled, turn upside-down on a cutting board, peel off the parchment paper, and use a good knife to cut off the edges from all sides. I like to put these into a ball jar, sealed tight, to use as a topping for vanilla ice cream. Then using a ruler, cut into 2-inch squares.

To store, wrap individually in plastic wrap, and place in layers between the parchment paper in a large plastic container. Store at room temperature or freeze.

Annie Epp's Raspberry Ice

Carol Moore *(Bayport, NY)*
Makes 2 quarts

My brothers and I were often bored when visiting my elderly aunt in Vermont every summer, but among the many bounties nature yielded to defray our boredom, none was so treasured by us as my aunt's neighbor Annie Epp's raspberry ice. The look and smell of fresh, red raspberries still takes me back to those summer afternoons with Annie Epp, a woman whose kindness and talent brought delight to three youngsters in the form of her raspberry ice.

Forty years after our summers in Vermont, I had lost touch with Annie Epp, but never with the memory of her frosty confection. So, one August day, when my own children were little and the raspberries were ripening, I located Annie Epp and wrote to her, asking for the recipe. In her letter of response was that precious recipe, valuable not just for the pleasure it brought, but for what it could still bring. I have only made the raspberry ice a few times since then, and, though I have it still, I think just having the recipe in my file box is often comfort enough.

3 cups sugar
2 quarts raspberries
2 cups water
¼ teaspoon sea salt
1 teaspoon lemon juice

Sprinkle sugar over the raspberries. Let set for 2 hours, and then mash the berries, add water, bring to a boil, and let cool. Strain through cheesecloth to catch any seeds. Taste, and if not sweet enough, add more sugar. Add salt and lemon juice, and then freeze in an ice cream freezer container until hard.

Temecula Olive Oil Company Gelato

Nancy Curry and Catherine Pepe, *Temecula Olive Oil Company (Temecula, CA)*

6 egg yolks
1 cup sugar
¼ cup Temecula Olive Oil Company D'Luscious Lemon
3 cups milk
1 cup heavy cream

Combine the egg yolks and sugar in the bowl of an electric mixer. Use the whip attachment to beat them for 5 minutes on medium speed or until the mixture is thick and very pale and forms a ribbon when the whip is lifted. Continue beating and drizzle in the olive oil; beat for 2 more minutes. Add the milk and cream, and continue to beat until all the ingredients are combined.

Freeze in an ice cream maker according to the manufacturer's instructions. For a great flavor sensation, make ice cream sandwiches, using the Temecula Olive Oil Company Lemon Cookie recipe (see page 140).

Italian Lemon Ice

Serves 8

My cousin's uncle surprised us one summer afternoon with his homemade lemon ice.

He served it right out of the metal container and scooped it into little white paper cups, just like the ones used when we were kids in Brooklyn at the Italian ice shops. He hasn't been feeling well lately, so he couldn't give me his recipe for this printing, but I asked around my old neighborhood and the flavor in this recipe is closest to his.

Story by Monica

2 cups sugar
8 cups water
1½ cups lemon juice, freshly squeezed
2 tablespoons lemon zest, finely chopped

Dissolve sugar in boiling water. Mix in lemon juice and zest. Cook to room temperature in a non-reactive metal container. Place in freezer, stirring every half hour, for 1½ - 2 hours or until frozen. Before serving, let stand for 5-10 minutes, then scoop into small pleated paper cups for that authentic Italian ice experience.

Hawaiian Wedding Cake

Lana Rae Armitage *(Portsmouth, RI)*

2 cups flour
2 cups sugar
2 eggs
2 teaspoons baking soda
1 (8 oz.) can unsweetened crushed pineapples
1 cup walnuts, finely chopped

Icing

1 pound confectioner's sugar
1 (8 oz.) package cream cheese, softened
3 tablespoons butter, softened
1-2 tablespoons whole milk

Preheat an oven to 350°F. Put all the ingredients, except the nuts, in a bowl and mix. Pour the batter in a prepared pan, spray the sides and bottom of a 13- by 9- inch pan with baking spray, and place a piece of parchment paper on the bottom. Then spray, again.

Bake at 350°F for 45 minutes. Let cool before frosting.

Icing

Beat all the ingredients until you obtain a good consistency for spreading. Spread over the cooled cake and sprinkle with walnuts.

Cherry Pie

Serves 8-10

Pastry for 8-inch pie plate (see Pàte Brisée, page 19)
1 quart fresh cherries, pitted
1½ cups sugar
2 tablespoons flour

Using the pastry for an 8-inch pie plate, line and place the mixed fruit, sugar, and flour into the crust. Cover with a lattice crust, brushed lightly with egg white, and bake in a preheated 450°F oven for 20 minutes. Reduce the heat to 375°F and bake for an additional 15 minutes or until the crust is golden-brown. If using cherries that you have frozen, let stand overnight in the refrigerator to defrost; do not bake with frozen cherries.

Strawberry Shortcake

We all have our favorite birthday cakes, and since my birthday falls in the summer, mine has always been strawberry shortcake with strawberries that we have handpicked. Mostly other people buy or make it for me, but when I make it myself, I go back to the first recipe that I ever tried. Dennis used to make the dough, because I do not really have the patience that he had to make dough. I have also made it using a pound cake recipe or a simple white cake covered with strawberries and cream.

Story by Monica

Shortcake Dough

2 cups flour

5 teaspoons baking powder

½ teaspoon sea salt

3 tablespoons clover honey

½ cup Crisco® (although I have used extra virgin olive oil)

¾ cups milk

Topping

2 quarts fresh strawberries

1 pint whipping cream

1 teaspoon vanilla

Powdered sugar

Mix the first 4 ingredients and work in the shortening with a pastry knife. Add milk. Toss on a floured counter. Roll and cut with a large biscuit cutter; bake on a baking pan in a preheated 450°F oven for 15 minutes.

Topping

Whip cream and vanilla. Top shortcake with fresh whipped cream and several sliced or whole strawberries, sprinkled lightly with powdered sugar.

Blueberry Pie

Serves 8

> Coming home from Maine each summer, we would fill our cooler with pints of blueberries sold for $1 to $2 at the side of the road, in front of people's homes, on the honor system. Folks also sold smoked salmon, but you had to knock on the door to buy that. We would get home and try out all kinds of recipes, but blueberry pie was Dennis' favorite, next to blueberry pancakes.
>
> *Story by Monica*

Pie Crust

1½ cups sifted flour
½ teaspoon baking powder
½ teaspoon salt
¼ cup ice water (or more for desired texture)

Filling

6 cups fresh blueberries
½ cup sugar

3 tablespoons tapioca flour (add another ½ tablespoon for a firmer filling)
¼ teaspoon cinnamon
2 tablespoons lemon juice, freshly squeezed
2 tablespoons unsalted butter
1 egg white (for brushing top crust)

Pie Crust

Sift together the flour, baking powder, and salt. Mix in water to shape dough until firm enough to roll. Line pie plate with the dough.

Filling

Wash blueberries and remove stems. Drain and dry completely on paper towels. Mix sugar, tapioca, and cinnamon, then add the blueberries and lemon juice until all the blueberries are coated. Pour into a 9-inch pie crust and dot with butter. Cover with thin top crust or lattice top. Brush top crust with egg white to prevent burning. Bake in a 400°F oven for the first 12 minutes, then reduce heat to 350°F and bake another 40 minutes or until filling is bubbling and thickened and crust is golden brown.

Pavlova

Peggy Bryant *(Brooklyn, NY)*
Serves 6

Peggy shared with us her sister-in-law Jill's adaptation of an old recipe that she enjoyed in England, but adapted for use in her Australian kitchen. Oddly, all of the native Aussies say that it is the best that they have ever tasted. Serve with any sliced summery fruit for an extra treat.

Story by Mary Elizabeth

Pavlova

4 egg whites
8 ounces superfine sugar
1 teaspoon white wine vinegar
1 teaspoon corn starch

Filling

6 ounces heavy cream (use British double cream, available at specialty stores)
1 tablespoon confectioner's sugar
1 tablespoon marsala or dry sherry (optional)
9 ounces mascarpone cheese, room temperature
4 ounces strawberries, sliced
4 ounces raspberries, sliced
1 ripe peach, sliced ,

Pavlova

Preheat the oven to 275°F. Spray a cookie sheet generously with baking spray. Line with parchment paper. Place a 9-inch dinner plate on it, and trace a circle using confectioner's sugar.

In a large, dry bowl, whisk the egg whites until they form stiff peaks.

Gradually whisk in the superfine sugar, a tablespoon at a time, until the mixture becomes thick and glossy. Then carefully fold in the white wine vinegar and the corn starch.

Spoon half the mixture on the baking paper to fill the circle. Then drop large spoonfuls of the remaining mixture on top, adding more to the edges to form a high rim.

Place the meringue in the center of the oven. After 5 minutes, lower to 250°F. Bake for 50 minutes, and then turn the oven off without opening the door. Leave the meringue in the oven for at least 3 hours or overnight to cool completely. Transfer to a wire rack and remove the parchment paper. Place in a large serving bowl.

Filling

Whip the cream with the confectioner sugar's, and then fold in the marsala or sherry and the mascarpone. Spoon into the meringue case and pile the fruit on top. Keep cool, but do not refrigerate before serving.

Chef's Tips

The Perfect Meringue Every Time

Set the temperature of the oven very low (before starting, test your oven temperature by hanging an oven thermometer in the oven and compare it with the temperature that you set it at; by doing so, you can ensure that the meringue cooks slowly).

Use eggs whites at room temperature; never straight from the refrigerator.

When cracking the eggs, be careful not to leave any trace of yolk in the whites.

Whisk the whites in a spotless, dry bowl: the slightest trace of grease will prevent them from whisking to full volume.

The egg whites must be whisked well between additions of sugar. If you rush this stage, a syrupy liquid may separate out.

The addition of white wine vinegar or lemon juice and corn starch will ensure that the meringue turns out soft and fluffy inside.

Meringue can be flavored by adding coarsely grated chocolate, ground or chopped hazelnuts, almonds, or other nuts. If you toast nuts before adding, it will enhance the flavor. Another option is to use finely grated orange or lemon zest to give the meringue a nice zing.

Tips for a Well-Stocked Pantry

It is always best to use fresh vegetables, meats, and fish, but in a pinch, you may have to rely on your stored ingredients. Try to keep the following items stocked in your pantry, refrigerator, and freezer, so, you can cook up a tasty and healthy meal any time. It is also a good idea to stock up when these items are on sale at your supermarket. Always remember to check the expiration date on sale items.

Basics for a Quick Meal

In the Pantry: pastas (different grains, shapes, and sizes), several kinds of rice, oatmeal, and other cereals, seasoned bread crumbs, stuffing mix, several varieties of beans (dried and canned), canned tomatoes (whole, crushed, puréed, and paste), teriyaki sauce, Gravy Master®, chicken and beef stocks, canned milk, dried mushrooms, various nuts, different kinds of flour (white, whole wheat, rye, cake, gluten-free), sugars (brown, raw, white, confectioner's), molasses, honey, baking soda/powder, vanilla (and other essences like lemon and orange), chocolate, caramel and peanut butter chips, dried fruits (raisins, cherries, cranberries, apricots, pineapples, mangos), peanut butter, and sprinkles

Dried Spices: ground cinnamon, nutmeg, whole and ground cloves, garlic and onion powders and pieces, crystallized and ground ginger, chili powder, paprika, cumin, curry powder, garam masala, coriander, and different kinds of salt and pepper

Dried Herbs: oregano, parsley, dill, ground and whole rosemary, basil, cilantro, mint, sage, bay leaves, and thyme

In the Freezer: several kinds of vegetables and fruits, including peppers, onions, celery, cherries, berries, bananas, raspberries and peaches; frozen juices from citrus fruits kept in ice trays; pizza dough;

cheese; butter; cookie dough; leftover stock (vegetable, fish, chicken); sauces; and bits of meats, peeled shrimp, and fish fillets

In the Refrigerator: lemon, lime, and orange juice; any leftovers from open bottles of wine, beer, and champagne to use in a recipe; capers; sun-dried tomatoes; olives; relish; horseradish; marmalade and jams; and a variety of bottled sauces for flavoring, including chili sauce, hoisin, teriyaki, soy, and barbeque

Growing Your Own Herbs

Most of us are ambitious gardeners, and we end up buying and growing more herbs than we can possibly use. So, before you plant your garden, be sure to carefully plan how much you will need to grow. Here is a sampling of the basics for every herb garden:

- Basil
- Chives
- Coriander (also known as cilantro)
- Dill
- Mint
- Oregano
- Parsley
- Rosemary
- Thyme

Once you have harvested your herbs, you will need to decide whether you will be using them within the next week or not.

For short-term use: for the storage of basil, parsley, and cilantro, you can trim the ends, place in a glass with an inch of water on the counter at room temperature for up to a week, clipping for each use each time that you need them. For chives, thyme, and rosemary, loosely cover the unrinsed herbs in plastic wrap, and place in the warmest part of the refrigerator or in a large plastic bag with a crumpled paper towel. Rinse them immediately before using.

If you will not be using your herbs right away, they can be dried for future use. To dry, either place chopped basil, parsley leaves, or whole thyme or rosemary on a plate. Set aside in a cool, dry place for several days, and then store them in a plastic container in the freezer or refrigerator. You can also make small bouquets of herbs tied with ribbon or string, and hang them upside-down to dry, then storing them as mentioned above or displaying them in your kitchen for a homey touch. Use your frozen herbs right up until your next growing season.

Growing Your Own Food

Healthy living does not mean giving up good food and great flavor. Simply eating unprocessed food and employing healthy cooking methods will put you on track for better overall health. Serving fresh garlic, green, leafy vegetables like spinach and kale, herbs like basil and parsley, and using extra virgin olive oil for sautéing and salad dressings are all great ways to improve and maintain a healthier lifestyle.

Growing some of your own vegetables and fruits has the added benefit of saving money and increasing quality family time by working together in the garden. Blueberries and raspberries are easy to grow, and can be great options for beginning gardeners. In warmer climates, citrus fruits grow in many a backyard. Monica's Italian vegetable garden is comprised of herbs such as oregano, basil, and parsley, along with cherry, plum, and beef-steak tomatoes, eggplant, and green and red peppers. We eat what is most plentiful as it is picked, and then prepare by canning or freezing the rest of the herbs, fruits, and veggies for future use.

Grilling Tips

Grilling a Whole Chicken, Turkey, Duck, or Goose

For chicken and turkey, remove the giblets and reserve for gravy. Rinse the bird and pat dry with paper towels. Tuck the wing tips under the back, and tie the legs together with kitchen string. Brush the chicken or turkey with extra virgin olive oil or butter, and salt and pepper inside and out. For duck or goose, season inside and out with salt and pepper, make a cut between the wing joints and back, as there will be an excess of fat to drain off during cooking, and then pierce the skin all over. Place the bird on a roasting rack, breast-side-up, in a heavy-gauge foiled pan with ½ cup of water, and cook on medium-high heat. Place on the cooking grate, close the cover, and grill. If using a thermometer, grill until the internal temperature reaches 180°F in the thickest part of the thigh and 170°F in the breast. For turkey, duck, and goose, cut the string holding the legs ⅔ through the cooking time. After transferring to a serving platter, let stand for 10 minutes before carving. If making gravy for chicken, remove the bird from the pan and place directly on the grate for 15 minutes prior to the end of cooking time; for turkey, remove the bird from the pan and place on the grate for 30 minutes prior to the end of cooking time. Make your favorite gravy as you would for an oven-roasted bird. If using barbeque sauce, brush on 30 minutes before the end of cooking time, as it tends to burn if put on too soon.

4-5-pound chicken: grill for approximately 1½ hours; serves 2-4

10-12-pound turkey: grill for 11-13 minutes per pound; serves 10-12

4-5-pound duck: grill for approximately 1½-2 hours; serves 2-4

10-12-pound goose: grill for approximately 2½-3 hrs; serves 4-6

Grilling a Whole Fish (Such as Bluefish, Red Snapper, or Rainbow Trout)

Clean and scale fish. Season inside and out with salt and pepper and brush with butter. Wrap in aluminum foil and place directly on the grilling grate, using medium heat for 30 minutes (about a 2-pound fish) to 1 hour (about a 4-6-pound fish). Cooking time depends on the size of the fish. Use a double thickness of aluminum foil if you are stuffing the fish. A basic stuffing of onion, celery, parsley, and butter is suitable for many kinds of fish, and adds a wonderful flavor. You can bulk up the basic stuffing by adding bread crumbs or rice.

Roasting a Pig
By Chef Gregory Lupo

Grill: The temperature at the roast should be kept constant at around 200-250°F. Split the rib bones at the spine to allow the pig to lay flat, being careful not to pierce the skin. Fill the grill with charcoal, and burn until it has turned ash-gray. Place heavy wire the size of the pig over the grill, 13 inches from the coals. Place the pig flat, skin-side-up, on the wire surface. Place a second wire over the pig, sandwiching the pig between the 2 layers of wire.

Rotisserie: If using a rotisserie, make sure that the weight is evenly distributed. Follow the directions from your rotisserie manual.

Rock-lined Pit: Dig a hole 2 ½-3 feet deep at the center with a diameter of 5-7 feet, depending on the size of the pig. Line the pit with rocks. Light a fire. Additional small, round rocks should be placed in the fire to be heated. As the fire burns down, wet the burlap and dress the pig as desired. Place the pig on chicken wire. Under the legs, make slits big enough to insert round, heated rocks. When the rocks are very hot, use tongs to fill the abdominal cavity and slits. Tie the front legs together, and then the back legs. Wrap the pig in chicken wire, fastening well, so it can be lifted. Completely cover the ashy coals and rocks with corn stalks and leaves or grass trimmings. Lower the pig onto the leaves. Cover it generously on top with some of the leaves. Place the wet burlap over leaves to hold the heat, and steam the pig. Cover with a large canvas. Shovel dirt or gravel over canvas to keep the steam in.

General Note for Grilling, Rotisserie, or Pit: Always check the internal temperature with a meat thermometer. Once the internal temperature reaches 160°F, the meat should be removed. A good place to check is the ham, as it is the largest section. Time is a variant; check often. Once cooked, an estimated 1-2 hours will keep the pig warm without drying out.

Cooking on the Grill: For estimated grilling time, see Grilling Chart 1 below.. Turn over half-way through the cooking process.

Cooking via Rotisserie: Place pig 12 inches away from the source of the heat. Keep the heat constant.

Cooking via Pit: Estimated cooking times are 2 hours for a 25-pound live weight, 2 ½ hours for a 50-pound live weight, 4 hours for a 75-pound live weight, and 8 hours for a 150-pound live weight. When in doubt, leave it in the pit for a big longer. The pig will not burn, as it is cooked by the steam. Start cooking 12 hours ahead of the serving time, depending on the chart below.

Grilling Chart 1

Weight of Pig	Charcoal	Amount of Gas	Wood	Cooker Temperature	Estimated Cooking Time with Closed Lid
75 pounds	60 pounds	40-pound cylinder	1/3 cord	225-250°F	6-7 hours
100 pounds	70 pounds	40-pound cylinder	1/3-1/2 cord	225-250°F	7-8 hours
125 pounds	80 pounds	40-pound cylinder	1/2 cord	225-250°F	8-9 hours

Grlling Chart 2: Estimating Serving Sizes from Dressed Pig

75 pounds of dressed pig	30 pounds of cooked, chopped pork
100 pounds of dressed pig	40 pounds of cooked, chopped pork
125 pounds of dressed pig	50 pounds of cooked, chopped pork
14 pounds of uncooked shoulder	10 pounds cooked
6-7 pounds of uncooked Boston butt	3 pounds cooked
14 pounds of uncooked ham	6-7 pounds cooked

Chef's Tips by Chef Nicole Roarke

Grilling

Grilling is the process in which food is cooked from radiant heat located below a grate or grill rack to create a delicious charred flavor and appearance. This quick cooking technique is best used with tender cuts of meat and poultry, which are trimmed of excess fat and connective tissue (for example, burgers, baby rack of lamb chops, pork tenderloin, New York strip steak, flank steak, and chicken breasts). Fish may also be grilled, but most chefs would agree that firm fish such as swordfish, tuna, mako shark, and salmon are easier to maneuver on the grill.

The high heat and intense flavor also makes grilling an ideal method to cook vegetables. Softer vegetables such as zucchini, summer squash, eggplant, and onions may be placed directly on the grill when raw. For harder vegetables (such as fennel, sweet potatoes, and carrots), par-cook them ahead of time before grilling.

In order to enhance the flavor of the meat, fish, poultry, or vegetables, you may choose a marinade or a dry spice rub of your liking. For a simpler approach, just use kosher salt and freshly cracked black pepper.

One important tip to remember when grilling is to always have a hot, preheated grill. If the grill is not hot enough, the food will stick to the grates. Also, you should always have a clean grill, because any leftover food particles on the grates will burn and give your food a bitter taste.

Barbeque

It is a common misconception that grilling and barbequing is the same thing. A barbeque grill is the device that we use to grill food, and is most commonly found in backyards, at picnic grounds, and on some beaches. The type of food known as "barbeque" and the cooking technique called "barbequing" refers to a Southern style of cooking meat very slowly over a fire pit using dry and wet rubs known as barbeque sauce. The best cuts of meat for barbeque are mostly on the bone, such as pork and beef ribs or chicken on the bone.

Kitchen Must-haves

When arriving home from the grocery store, spend an additional twenty minutes properly storing your food. Place a colander in the sink and a cutting board on the counter, and then grab your plastic storage containers. Begin washing the vegetables and fruit in the colander, using your discretion on which items can be left whole (e.g., apples), while others can be "broken down" (heads of broccoli can be cut into florets). Chefs refer to "breaking down" as the trimming and cutting of ends, roots, leaves, skins, outer layers, and stalks. By saving the unusable celery roots, carrot peels, and pepper stems, for instance, you can prepare your own vegetable and chicken stock at a later date.

By purchasing whole vegetables or buying them in bulk and breaking them down yourself, you save money and can control the quality of your homemade stock, rather than using store-bought stock. When you are about to prepare a recipe, the majority of your vegetables are now ready. This initial twenty minutes spent storing your produce will help you save time the day before preparing for dinner, parties, or events.

For example, after washing the head of broccoli, cut the florets and store them in the refrigerator in a plastic container or a large plastic bag, so, it is ready to eat. Keep the stems and stalks in a large bowl designated as your "stock bin." Continue breaking down the rest of your vegetables, so, your refrigerator is filled with cleaned, cut, and easily accessible vegetables, as well as a full "stock bin" for making homemade stock.

It is also helpful to use this method when purchasing and storing your proteins. Rather than putting ten pounds of chicken in your refrigerator (which may spoil before you can use it), open the package, individually wrap each piece, and place them in large freezer bags. Determine how much to store in your refrigerator for immediate use, and place the remaining individual bags in the freezer to be taken out for a later date.

Basic Recipe for Vegetable Stock

Makes 2 quarts

1. Fill a stock or large sauce-pot with vegetable trimmings from your stock bin.
2. Be sure to include 1 yellow onion, 2 carrots, 1 bunch of celery, and fresh herbs, including (but not limited to) bay leaf, thyme, parsley stems, rosemary, and peppercorns.
3. Add cold water (just covering the vegetables), bring to a boil, and immediately reduce to a simmer. Simmer for 1 hour.
4. Remove from the heat and let cool for 30 minutes.
5. Strain contents through a colander, and then a second time through a fine-mesh strainer called a chinois.
6. If you prefer a darker stock, add 2 tablespoons of tomato paste and any tomato trimmings you have.

Note: most chefs agree not to salt the stock. Use the stock as a basic foundation for a soup or sauce that can be further flavored or salted later. This way, you can control the amount of salt that goes into the finished product.

Basic Recipe for Chicken Stock

Makes 2 quarts

1. Fill a large stock-pot with raw or cooked chicken, gizzards, bones, trimmings, and neck – do not use internal organs (e.g., liver or kidneys).
2. Add cold water to just cover the chicken parts and vegetable trimmings from your stock bin. Be sure to include 1 yellow onion, 2 carrots, 1 bunch of celery, and fresh herbs, including (but not limited to) bay leaf, thyme, parsley stems, rosemary, and peppercorns.
3. Allow to simmer for at least 1 hour, but no more than 2 hours.
4. Remove from the heat. Allow it to cool for 30 minutes.
5. Strain contents through a colander, and then a second time through a fine-mesh strainer called a chinois. If the stock is for immediate use, skim off any excess fat from the top of the stock with a large spoon or ladle and discard. If the stock is to be used at a later date, cool in the refrigerator: the fat will rise to the top

and solidify, which can easily be removed with a large spoon before use.

6. If you prefer a dark stock, coat the chicken bone with vegetable oil, and roast in an oven for approximately 20 to 30 minutes at 350°F until a brown color is achieved. Then proceed as above, but include an 8-ounce can of tomato paste and any tomato trimmings that you have.

Now, it is up to you to season with salt to taste. Otherwise, use as a flavor foundation.

Mise en Place

Mise en place [MEEZ-ahn-plahs] is a French term that literally means "setting in place." Mise en place refers to a chef's set-up of essential ingredients and tools that are necessary to begin the actual cooking process. Before beginning any recipe, it is important to:

1. Have all the ingredients and equipment readily accessible.
2. Read the entire recipe and make sure that you understand all of the instructions and steps that you need to follow.
   If your mise en place is set out and organized right in front of you, it allows for a steady flow of production. Essentially, organization leads to less error. For most professional and at-home chefs, a mise en place consists of:
   - Kosher salt: keep readily accessible in a small finger pot.
   - Freshly cracked black pepper: keep in a refillable pepper mill with whole black peppercorns.
   - Blended oil: olive oil alone tends to be strong in flavor, expensive, and cannot withstand high cooking heat. By adding oil such as vegetable, canola, or soybean, you can create your own blended oil. I follow a three to one ratio: three-parts light or neutral oil such as canola or vegetable (corn or soybean work just as well) to one-part extra virgin olive oil.
3. Flour/corn starch: not only is flour or corn starch essential for baking, they oftentimes act as a thickening agent, if necessary. Roux is equal parts flour to fat: for example, 1 cup of all-purpose flour to 1 cup of melted butter. Whisk together over low heat until

it is sandy in color and similar to peanut butter in consistency. By this time, all the raw flour taste is cooked out. This takes approximately 5 minutes. By adding a roux to a sauce or soup and bringing it to a boil, you can thicken it instantly.

Slurry is a mix of ½ cup of corn starch with ¼-½ cup of cold water until a heavy cream consistency is reached. Bring your recipe (e.g., sauce or soup) to a boil, and whisk in the slurry. Return to a simmer (5-7 minutes). If you add corn starch directly to your recipe, it will clump and not alter the thickness, which is why it is necessary to mix the corn starch with water or any flavorful liquid (such as wine, stock, or juice) ahead of time before adding it to your recipe.

4. Sugar/honey: just as a pinch of salt is added to almost all baking recipes to bring out the sweetness and balance the flavor, I add a pinch of sugar or tablespoon of honey to my savory soups and sauces. I believe that it creates a well-rounded depth of flavor.

5. Roasted garlic: there are two ways to roast garlic:
   - Cut a quarter off the top of a whole bulb of garlic.
   - Drizzle with oil, salt, and pepper.
   - Place bulb in the center of a large, square piece of aluminum foil. Bring the corners up around the bulb, and pinch closed at the top.
   - Place the foil onto a sheet tray.
   - Roast "low and slow" at 300°F for 45 minutes until fragrant and soft.
   - Remove from the oven, open the foil, and allow it to cool.
   - Squeeze the individual cloves out of the bulb.

   OR
   - Place 1 cup of whole, peeled garlic cloves in a medium sauce-pot.
   - Pour blended oil over the garlic until it is just covered (approximately 2 cups).
   - Place the pot over medium to low heat (the oil should be lower than a simmer). After 20-30 minutes, the garlic should be soft, fragrant, and slightly gold in color.
   - Allow the garlic to cool.

6. Blended herb oil (makes a great gift): place oil in a decorative bottle, tie a ribbon around the neck, and add a holiday sticker on the front, or, write the recipe on a holiday recipe card to make it a gift that "keeps giving," as my good friend Dawn says.

    - Place 1 cup of tightly packed fresh herbs (such as basil, dill, or a combination, such as ½ cup of sage and ½ cup of thyme) in a blender or food processor. Be sure to use only the leaves, discarding all the stems.
    - Add 1 teaspoon of kosher salt and 1/8 teaspoon of freshly cracked black pepper.
    - Pulse herbs, salt, and pepper to rough chop.
    - Add blended oil to cover and purée.

You can either leave the herbs in the oil for a stronger flavor and more rustic appearance, or, you can strain the oil with a fine-mesh strainer or chinois (cone-shaped strainer). The oil retains a beautiful light-green color, and should be very fragrant and delicious. Use as a dipping oil for fresh bread, as a dressing for a fresh mozzarella and plum tomato salad, as a drizzle on a plate, or on top of a puréed soup.

You can also add the herb oil to mayonnaise to create an herb aioli for potato salad. Add to cream and serve over pasta. The possibilities are endless and always delicious.

When cutting up apples to serving on a cheese platter or when using for dipping into a fondue: to prevent the apple from oxidizing after you cut them, make a "citrus bath," which is essentially an anti-browning solution. Squeeze the juice of 1 lemon into 2 cups of water, and place your sliced apples in the solution until ready to serve.

Baker's Tips

Have you ever tasted something that you absolutely loved, but when you got the recipe and attempted to reproduce it, you could not come up with the same results? Baking is a precise science. You cannot deviate from the directions – when they say "do not over beat," they mean it. If you follow the directions exactly, you will be surprised at the results.

Read your recipe from start to finish. Every baker can tell you a story of leaving out a key ingredient when they were distracted or multitasking, as many of us do. Or, after beginning their recipe, they got to the end and read that it must chill for three hours, and their guests were arriving to eat in one hour.

Preheat your oven. If you are unsure if your oven is accurate, purchase a small oven thermometer so you can double-check that the temperature you set on your oven is the same as the thermometer reading; if not, you will need to adjust accordingly.

Mise en place all your ingredients before you begin. It is important to use your measuring cup for flour, but remember to level it off and use a knife to tap the top of the cup, making sure that it settles.

Use a cooking scale to weigh your dry ingredients and a measuring cup with a spout to measure your liquid ingredients.

Eggs and butter must be brought to room temperature. If you see these ingredients in your recipe, you should start by placing your eggs on a dinner plate on your counter-top. Then take the amount of butter that you need, cut it into tablespoons, and put it on your counter. The room air will soften it up, so, when it is time to actually start the recipe, it has come to the perfect consistency.

Buy good-quality chocolate, vanilla, and cinnamon. Whenever I shop, I make sure to stop in the baking aisle of the store to buy chocolate when it is on sale to keep my pantry well-stocked. Whenever possible, I also use Vietnamese cinnamon, because it is sweeter and much more flavorful.

Use fresh spices and herbs whenever possible. It will make all the difference in the taste.

Baking Must-have Ingredients
- Salt, baking powder, baking soda, and instant oatmeal
- All-purpose (also known as "AP") flour
- All types of chocolate: white, dark, semisweet, and unsweetened
- Salted, sweet butter
- Eggs
- Whole milk and heavy cream
- Vanilla
- Sugars: raw, confectioner's, white, and both dark and light brown
- Molasses, and dark and light corn syrups
- Silver beads, red, green and white sprinkles, and sugar crystals

Baking Must-have Equipment
- Zester
- Several sets of individual measuring cups and spoons
- Two Pyrex® measuring cups
- Small preparation bowls or Pyrex® custard cups
- Three each of cutting boards, good-quality cookie sheets, and cooling racks
- One large and small cookie scoop
- Variety of cookie cutters (seasonal/holiday and shapes)
- Four mixing bowls (of various sizes)
- Cuisinart®
- Hand-mixer
- Whisk, spatulas (all sizes), wooden spoons, and a ruler
- Good-quality knife (for chopping nuts and chocolate)
- Hand-sifter*
- Pastry brush

*Be sure to read the recipe directions carefully. If it calls for "sifted flour," you should sift the flour before measuring. If it calls for "flour, sifted," however, you must measure first, and then sift the flour.

Menu Planner

One of the first things that you should do when starting to plan a menu for a special event or holiday is to get out all of your favorite cookbooks, recipe file boxes, and any other recipe collections that you have created.

Here is the process for recipe collection that Mary Elizabeth has developed over the past thirty years: as I go through the culinary magazines that I receive each month, I fold over any pages with recipes that I want to try. After I have thoroughly savored the magazine, I tear out those pages and place them into an accordion folder, which contains tabs for each course (breakfast, lunch, snack, dinner, dessert, etc.).

When I am ready to start planning a menu, I sit at the kitchen table while sipping on my morning coffee, and begin hunting thorough my vast collection of recipes. I first list all the dishes that I have selected for each course. Once I am confident that the tastes and flavors go together, and that everything fits well with my theme for that event, I start the shopping list, which is divided into categories such as produce, dairy, and meats to make it easier when I am shopping.

After I have methodically gone through each recipe and jotted down the ingredients, I then take my list and look in my pantry for any items that I may already have. Before leaving the house to start my shopping, I also list any miscellaneous items that I will need to get from specialty stores, such as the flower shop or party store. This method has served me well over the years.

The first time that I try a new recipe, I typically follow it exactly as written. If I like the recipe and it is well-received by my family or company, it gets pulled out of the accordion folder, and is typed on my computer, where I add any notes that I have taken along the way (e.g., a different technique that I have used, a short-cut, or variations in ingredients). Then I file it on my hard drive in a recipe folder with subfolders for each course. I love to share recipes with others, so I can easily send them in an e-mail.

Afterward, I print the recipe and place it in my "keeper" binder, with tabs for each course (I have affectionately used the term "keeper" ever since I borrowed it from my husband and sons, who use it to describe whatever fish that they take home after a fishing trip).

My binder is not fancy, but I have made sure to use one that has a clear, plastic sleeve on the front. When I start prepping to make a recipe, I pull it out of the binder, place it under the plastic sleeve, and stand it on my counter. Needless to say, the plastic sleeve inevitably gets splattered, but can easily be wiped off with a sponge, keeping the recipe intact so it can be filed away, again. This process continues as I often find myself making notes on the recipes (for example, if I find a particular brand that makes a difference in the flavor, or, if I substitute or add a new ingredient).

When planning a menu, you should keep in mind the following key questions:

How many guests will I be expecting?
Whether it is a party of fifty or a dinner for you and your spouse, the number of guests is important to determine before grocery-shopping for your food and fare.

What is my budget?
Certain food items are more expensive than others, so, planning meals with lower-cost ingredients will help you stick to your budget without sacrificing quality.

What is my concept or theme?
Like great music, each component of a great dish should be in harmony with one another. The whole meal should make sense. If it is a Mexican fiesta, Italian pasta night, or a New Year's Eve cocktail party, you should keep the menu items synchronized to ensure that the flavors will mesh well together. Creating a concept or theme for your event menu will keep you, the chef, focused within these guidelines, and prevent you from feeling overwhelmed. Balancing flavors, colors, and textures goes hand-in-hand with deciding which recipes complement each other.

Do my guests have any dietary restrictions or limitations?
For example, one of your guests may be a vegetarian, diabetic, or is allergic to nuts or shellfish. Knowing what your guests can and cannot have will guarantee an enjoyable meal. It may also be helpful to keep notes on an index card in your recipe box, where you list your guests' names and their dietary restrictions, as well as their likes and dislikes.

Finally, do not overwhelm your guests. Keep it simple and offer several choices, especially when planning a buffet. To give yourself more time with your guests, be sure to have everything out before anyone arrives. Attractively display several cold appetizers and dips, decorative Sterno® dishes with meat and pasta entrées, and a large salad and basket of bread that complements your theme. You may also want to have the coffee urn ready to plug in, along with a selection of teas. For dessert, offer choices including fruit, chocolate, and something plain, such as pound cake or sugar cookies.

Years of hosting many dinner parties and family gatherings have gone into learning what goes well together. Below you will find menus comprised of recipes from each chapter that you can use to form a complete menu for you and your guests. Enjoy!

Menu Planners

Poolside Shower

Appetizer	Mexican Shrimp Cocktail (page 75), Lime Chicken Fingers (page 81, Salsa (page 87) and Guacamole (page 88) plus a basket of corn chips
Salad	Mesclun and Red-Leaf Lettuce Salad (page 55)
Entrée	New York Strip Steaks with Avocado Butter and Charred Corn Salsa (page 126), Pinchito de Mar (Grilled Seafood Skewer; page 119), and Pesto Bowtie Pasta (page 122)
Dessert	Cheesecake with Strawberry/Rhubarb Sauce (pages 136, 137 and Brownies (page 145)

Summer Meals

Appetizer	Clam Dip (page 85), Seafood Bisque (page 62), and Clams on the Half-Shell (page 73)
Salad	Arugula Salad with Pear and Bleu Cheese (page 54)
Entrée	Grilled Flat Iron Steaks with Sun-Dried Tomato Chimichurri (page 128)
Pasta	Shrimp and Pasta Salad (page 63)
Dessert	Strawberry Shortcake (page 152), Italian Lemon Ice (page 149), and Lemon Cookies (page 140)

Picnic Time

Appetizer	Bruschetta (page 90) and Caramelized Onion and Gruyere Tart (page 18)
Salad	Zesty Orange and Cucumber Salad (page 57) and Green Beans with Mustard and Shallot Vinaigrette (page 58)
Entrée	Old-Fashioned Southern Fried Chicken (page 104) and Tandoori Chicken (page 107)
Pasta	Linguine with Asparagus and Pine Nuts (page 123)
Dessert	Brownies (page 145) and Cherry Pie (page 151)

Backyard Barbeque

Appetizer	Mozzarella, Tomato, Red Onion Platter with Basil Drizzle (page 89)
Salad	Corn Salad (page 42), Creamy Cole Slaw (page 44), and Potato Salad (page 46)
Entrée	Barbeque Sauce and Chicken (page 105) and Deluxe Turkey Burgers (page 30)
Dessert	Chocolate Chip Cookies (page 144) and Raspberry and Peach Pie (page 138)

Request for Future Submissions

We have thoroughly enjoyed collecting these stories. As we received each story and recipe, we would anxiously read through and decide if it could be included in our book. We knew that it would be included if it evoked in us the emotions and memories that come to mind when we remember our own traditions. We reached out to family, friends, neighbors, and colleagues, and, now, we are reaching out to you, our readers. We would love to have you share your stories with us.

To do so, please send us the following information and e-mail your story to us at countrycomfortcookbooks@gmail.com, or, visit us on Facebook at "Country Comfort Cookbook." Please include your name, e-mail address, city, and state.

There is no word count or previous writing experience necessary, and we only require one rule: you write from your heart.

Thank you,

Mary Elizabeth and Monica

Resources

A heart-felt thanks goes out to our contributing chefs, cooks, and caterers for sharing their inspiration and works of art:

Carol Moore, www.cookingfreak.net

Chef Gregory Lupo and owner, Joseph Lupo, owfinefood.com

Chef Nick Suarez, www.thefoodexperiments.com

Chef Nicole Roarke, www.NRcatering.com

Christine Melcher, www.facebook.com/pages/
Sharing-Recipes/132481883433277

Darcy Grainger, www.DarcysDelights.com

Dee Fitzgerald, www.deefitzgerald.com

The Classic Catering People, www.classiccatering.com

Danny Glickberg and Chef Mitchel London, www.fairwaymarket.com

Nancy Curry and Catherine Pepe, Temecula Olive Oil Company (TOOC), www.temeculaoliveoil.com

Chef Tricia Wheeler, www.ediblecommunities.com/columbus/

www.ASilverwareAffair.net

About the Authors

Monica Musetti-Carlin holds a degree in liberal arts, and is an award-winning media consultant for a chain of newspapers on Long Island. As a journalist, lecturer, and "foodie" with over thirty years of experience in media, she continues to publish news and feature stories, advertorials, restaurant reviews, recipes; and advertising, copywriting, and public relations pieces for such publications as *The New York Times*, *New York Magazine*, and many New York weeklies. Through her advertising agency, she has had the opportunity to work with Jane Brody, Pete Seeger, and Yoko Ono. Monica has expanded her special events division, Eclectic Endeavors, to market and distribute her recipe and craft products. Most recently, in addition to writing the *Country Comfort* series, she is completing a work of fiction called *Park Slope* and several non-fiction projects.

Mary Elizabeth Roarke has her B.S. in nursing (1977), and has worked in the field for over thirty years. She now works in clinical research with a major pharmaceutical company. In 2008, she went to culinary school and earned a certificate in Pastry and Baking Arts. On weekends, she bakes alongside her daughter Nicole in their business, NR Catering, on Long Island, where she lives with her husband and their four children.

Mary Elizabeth has written a chapter for a book titled *Potluck Wisdom for the Pharmaceutical Professional*. This opportunity sparked her interest in writing, and she went on to combine her love of baking and sharing recipes in the cookbook series, *Country Comfort: Harvest, Holidays*, and *Slow-cooker*. She continues writing stories for local newspapers, works on her project's newsletter, and has published both scientific and professional articles. While at work, she started an e-mail recipe exchange called "Food for Thought," where she featured a weekly recipe received from colleagues all over the United States.

Since 2007, she has volunteered as a Board Member for BULA (Better Understanding of Life in Africa). Both for BULA and her full-time job, Mary Elizabeth collected and collated recipes for two charity cookbooks.

Index

A

Acierno, Bizzy, 123
Acierno, Dorothy, 32
Acierno, Kathy, 123
Angel-food Cake with Chocolate Shavings, 143
Annie Epp's Raspberry Ice, 147
Armitage, Lana Rae, 15, 150
Arugula Salad with Pear and Bleu Cheese, 54

B

Barbeque Sauce and Chicken, 105
Beef
    Grilled Flat Iron Steaks with Sun-Dried Tomato Chimichurri, 128
    New York Strip Steaks with Avocado Butter and Charred Corn Salsa, 126
Beverages
    Caribbean Cooler, 91
    Homemade Ginger Ale, 93
    Minty Mojitos, 94
    Strawberry-Raspberry Frozen Daquiris, 95
    Summer Punch, 92
Bird's Nest Eggs, 5
Blueberry
    Blueberry Lime Jam, 23
    Blueberry Picnic Cake, 21
    Blueberry Pie, 153
    Blueberry Whole-wheat Muffins, 10
Boger, Gerarda, 102
Bonilla, Chef Julian, 40
Bread and Butter Slices, 103
Breadcrumbs, 6
Brooklyn's Cheesiest Dog, 36
Brooklyn's Corniest Dog, 38
Brownies, 145
Bruschetta, 90
Bryant, Peggy, 154

C

Cambeiro, Chef Sebastian, 119
Caramelized Onion and Gruyere Tart, 18
Caribbean Cooler, 91
Carlin, Gretel, 85, 141
Cheesecake, 136
Cherry Pie, 151
Chicken

Barbeque Sauce and Chicken, 105
Basic Chicken Wings and Dipping Sauces, 82
Grilled Chicken, 106
Lime Chicken Fingers, 81
Old-Fashioned Southern Fried Chicken, 104
Spicy and Sweet Pan-fried Chicken, 108
Tandoori Chicken, 107
Chili
    Chili, Labor Day, 32
    Chili Dogs, Memorial Day, 33
Chocolate Chip Cookies, 144
Clam Chowder, North Fork, 61
Clam Dip, 85
Clams on the Half-Shell, 73
Cole Slaw
    Creamy, 44
    Sweet, 45
Corn Salad, 42
Cornish Hens, Fairway Market's, 114
Crepes with Berry Topping, 16
Créme Brûlée French Toast Topped with Fresh Strawberries, 12
Cromer, Kathy, 48
Cucumber
    Chilled Cucumber and Pickled Ginger Salad, 50
    Cucumber Salad, 49
    Zesty Orange and Cucumber Salad, 57
Curry, Nancy, 56, 57, 60, 78, 81, 84, 112, 121, 140, 148

D
Daquiris, Strawberry-Raspberry Frozen, 95
De Nicola, Robin, 11
De Santis, Lou, 66
Deluxe Turkey Burgers, 30
Dodge, Susan, 103

E
Eggs
    Bird's Nest Eggs, 5
    Garden Vegetable Omelet with Cheese, 7
    Elegant Watermelon Salad, 59
    Lox, Eggs and Onions, 8
Elegant Watermelon Salad, 59

F
Fairway Market
    Crab Cakes with Tartar Sauce, 86

    Grilled Cornish Game Hen, 114
    Grilled Red Snapper, 115
    Lamb Skewers with Yogurt Sauce, 110
    Lobster Roll, 29
Farrell, Chef Mike, 61
Fire-Roasted Mussels with Citrus Garlic Butter or Fresh Tomato Salsa, 79
Fish
    Grilled Red Snapper, 115
    Grilled Salmon, 117
    Grilled Swordfish with Spiced Red Pepper Sauce, 116
Fitzgerald, Dee, 82
Franklin, Chef Benny, 129
French Toast
    Crème Brulee French Toast, 12
    French Toast Bake with Summer Berries, 15
    Vanilla Almond Multi-grain French Toast, 13
 Fricke, Karen, 136

G
Garden Vegetable Omelet with Cheese, 7
Gazpacho, 60
Gelato, Temecula Olive Oil Company, 148
Ginger Ale, Homemade, 93
Glickberg, Danny, 29, 86, 110, 114, 115
Glick, Chef Andrea, 16
Grainger, Darcy, 51
Grandpa's Sauerkraut, 101
Greek Pasta Salad, 51
Green Beans with Mustard and Shallot Vinaigrette, 58
Grilled
    Deluxe Turkey Burgers, 30
    Grilled Basil Shrimp, 78
    Grilled Chicken, 106
    Grilled Cornish Game Hens, Fairway Market's, 114
    Grilled Fig, Brie, and Prosciutto Pizza, 34
    Grilled Flat Iron Steaks with Sun-Dried Tomato Chimichurri, 128
    Grilled Hearts of Romaine Drizzled with Dijon Vinaigrette, 53
    Grilled New York Strip Steaks with Avocado Butter and Charred Corn Salsa, 126
    Grilled Red Snapper, Fairway Market's, 115
    Grilled Salmon, 117
    Grilled Seafood Skewer (Pinchito de Mar), 119
    Grilled Swordfish with Spiced Red Pepper Sauce, 116
    Grilled Teriyaki Lamb Chops, 113
    Grilled Vegetable Pitas, 40
 Guacamole, 88

H
Hamburgers, Memorial Day, 31
Harding, Chef Therese, 67
Hawaiian Wedding Cake, 150
Holt, Chef Christopher, 50, 53, 79
Homemade Ginger Ale, 93
Homemade Waffles, 9

I
Ice Cream Cake, 141
Irene's Macaroni Salad, 48
Italian Lemon Ice, 149
Italian Pasta Salad, 64

J
Jamaican-Jerk Baked Beans, 102

K
Kim, Chef Shin, 108

L
Labor Day Chili, 32
Lamb
    Fairway Market's Lamb Skewers with Yogurt Sauce, 110
    Grilled Teriyaki Lamb Chops, 113
    Thai Grilled Leg of Lamb, 112
Lamia, Tom, 30
Larkin, Chef Richard, 62
Lemon Cookies, 140
Lime Chicken Fingers, 81
Linguine with Asparagus and Pine Nuts, 123
London, Chef Mitchel, 29, 86, 110, 114, 115
Longo, Linda, 54
Lox, Eggs, and Onions, 8
Lupo, Joseph and Chef Gregory, 160

M
Macaroni
    Macaroni and Cheese, Smoked Gouda, 131
    Macaroni and Cheese, Traditional, 129
    Macaroni Salad, All-American, 47
    Macaroni Salad, Irene Roarke's, 48
Marinara Sauce, 124
Mediterranean Wrap, 65
Mesclun and Red-Leaf Lettuce Salad, 55
Melcher, Christine, 106, 139

Memorial Day Hamburgers, 31
Mexican Shrimp Cocktail, 75
Meyers, Elizabeth, 47, 49, 64
Minty Mojitos, 94
Moore, Carol, 147
Mozzarella, Tomato and Red Onion Platter with Basil Drizzle, 89
Muffins
    Blueberry Whole-wheat Muffins, 10
    Whole-wheat Peaches and Cream Muffins, 11
Mussels, Fire-Roasted with Citrus Garlic Butter or Fresh Tomato Salsa, 79

N
North Fork Clam Chowder, 61
New York Strip Steaks with Avocado Butter and Charred Corn Salsa, 126

O
Old-Fashioned Southern Fried Chicken, 104
Ott, Amy, 113
Ott, Lorraine, 138, 143

P
Pàte Brisée, 19
Patterson, Jill, 45
Pavlova, 154
Pepe, Catherine, 56, 57, 60, 78, 81, 84, 112, 121, 140, 148
Pesto Bowtie Pasta, 122
Pinchito de Mar (Grilled Seafood Skewer), 119
Pollock, Chef Geraldine, 18, 20, 55
Potato Salad, 46
Prior, Susan, 65
Punch, Summer, 92

R
Raiser, Christian David, 42, 101, 105, 125
Raiser, Lena T., 21, 105
Raspberry
    Raspberry Ice, Auntie Epp's, 147
    Raspberry and Peach Pie, 138
Roarke, Chef Nicole, 142
Roasted Tomato and Shallot Marmalade, 67
Rosemary Shortbread Cookies, 84
Rosenberg, Lisa, 120
Ruder, Chef and Dr. Sonali, 34, 116, 126, 128

S
Saggio, Kate, 52
Salads

All-American Macaroni Salad, 47
Arugula Salad with Pear and Bleu Cheese, 54
Chilled Cucumber and Pickled Ginger Salad, 50
Corn Salad, 42
Cucumber Salad, 49
Greek Pasta Salad, 51
Green Beans with Mustard and Shallot Vinaigrette, 58
Grilled Hearts of Romaine Drizzled with Dijon Vinaigrette, 53
Irene Roarke's Macaroni Salad, 48
Italian Pasta Salad, 64
Mesclun and Red-Leaf Lettuce Salad, 55
Potato Salad, 46
Shrimp and Pasta Salad, 63
Strawberry Fig Basil Salad, 56
Summer Salad with Poppy Seed Dressing, 52
Watermelon Salad, Elegant, 59
Zesty Orange and Cucumber Salad, 57
Salsa, 87
Charred Corn Salsa, 126
Fresh Tomato Salsa, 79
Sauerkraut, Grandpa's, 101
Sausage and Cheese Breakfast, 20
Seafood
Clams on the Half-Shell, 73
Clam Chowder, North Fork, 61
Clam Dip, 85
Crab Cakes with Tartar Sauce, Fairway Market's, 86
Lobster Roll, Fairway Market's, 29
Fire-Roasted Mussels with Citrus Garlic Butter or Fresh Tomato Salsa, 79
Grilled Basil Shrimp, 78
Grilled Red Snapper, 115
Grilled Salmon, 117
Grilled Seafood Skewer (Pinchito de Mar), 119
Grilled Swordfish with Spiced Red Pepper Sauce, 116
Mexican Shrimp Cocktail, 75
Seafood Bisque, 62
Shrimp and Pasta Salad, 63
Tuscan Summer Shrimp Cocktail, 76
Sicilian Summer Pasta Sauce, 125
Silverware Affair, 59, 75, 76, 131
Smith, Carol, 23
Smoked Gouda Mac n' Cheese, 131
Soup
Clam Chowder, North Fork, 61
Gazpacho, 60
Seafood Bisque, 62
Southwestern Stew, 66

Spicy and Sweet Pan-fried Chicken, 108
Steak
    Grilled Flat Iron Steaks with Sun-Dried Tomato Chimichurri, 128
    New York Strip Steaks with Avocado Butter and Charred Corn Salsa, 126
Stone Fruit Torte, 142
Strawberry
    Strawberry Fig Basil Salad, 56
    Strawberries Napoleon, 139
    Strawberry-Raspberry Frozen Daiquiris, 95
    Strawberry and Rhubarb Sauce, 137
    Strawberry Shortcake, 152
Suarez, Chef Nick, 36, 38
Sullivan, Elizabeth, 132
Summer Garden Zucchini Carpaccio, 120
Summer Punch, 92
Summer Salad with Poppy Seed Dressing, 52

T
Tandoori Chicken, 107
Temecula Olive Oil Company Gelato, 148
Thai Peanut Noodles, 121
Thai Grilled Leg of Lamb, 112
Traditional Macaroni and Cheese, 129
Turkey Burgers, Deluxe, 30
Tuscan Summer Shrimp Cocktail, 76

V
Vanilla Almond Multigrain French Toast Topped with Summer Berries, 13

W
Waffles, Homemade, 9
Watermelon Salad, Elegant, 59
Watkins Thoburn, Marguerite, 46
Wheeler, Chef Tricia, 19
White, Kathleen, 13
Whole-wheat Peaches and Cream Muffins, 11

Z
Zesty Orange and Cucumber Salad, 57
Zucchini, Summer Garden Carpaccio, 120

My Recipes

My Recipes

My Recipes

My Recipes

My Recipes

My Recipes

My Recipes

My Recipes